THE
COMPLETE
IDIOT'S
GUIDE® TO

Working Less, Earning More

by Jeff Cohen

ALPHA

A member of Penguin Group (USA) Inc.

For Carol, my muse and soul mate forever and a day.

ALPHA BOOKS

Published by the Penguin Group

Penguin Group (USA) Inc., 375 Hudson Street, New York, New York 10014, USA

Penguin Group (Canada), 90 Eglinton Avenue East, Suite 700, Toronto, Ontario M4P 2Y3, Canada (a division of Pearson Penguin Canada Inc.)

Penguin Books Ltd., 80 Strand, London WC2R 0RL, England

Penguin Ireland, 25 St. Stephen's Green, Dublin 2, Ireland (a division of Penguin Books Ltd.)

Penguin Group (Australia), 250 Camberwell Road, Camberwell, Victoria 3124, Australia (a division of Pearson Australia Group Pty. Ltd.)

Penguin Books India Pvt. Ltd., 11 Community Centre, Panchsheel Park, New Delhi—110 017, India

Penguin Group (NZ), 67 Apollo Drive, Rosedale, North Shore, Auckland 1311, New Zealand (a division of Pearson New Zealand Ltd.)

Penguin Books (South Africa) (Pty.) Ltd., 24 Sturdee Avenue, Rosebank, Johannesburg 2196, South Africa

Penguin Books Ltd., Registered Offices: 80 Strand, London WC2R 0RL, England

Copyright © 2008 Jeff Cohen

International Standard Book Number: 978-1-59257-798-9
Library of Congress Catalog Card Number: 2008922785

10   09   08   8   7   6   5   4   3

Interpretation of the printing code: The rightmost number of the first series of numbers is the year of the book's printing; the rightmost number of the second series of numbers is the number of the book's printing. For example, a printing code of 08-1 shows that the first printing occurred in 2008.

Printed in the United States of America

Note: This publication contains the opinions and ideas of its author. It is intended to provide helpful and informative material on the subject matter covered. It is sold with the understanding that the author and publisher are not engaged in rendering professional services in the book. If the reader requires personal assistance or advice, a competent professional should be consulted.

The author and publisher specifically disclaim any responsibility for any liability, loss, or risk, personal or otherwise, which is incurred as a consequence, directly or indirectly, of the use and application of any of the contents of this book.

Most Alpha books are available at special quantity discounts for bulk purchases for sales promotions, premiums, fund-raising, or educational use. Special books, or book excerpts, can also be created to fit specific needs.

For details, write: Special Markets, Alpha Books, 375 Hudson Street, New York, NY 10014.

Publisher: *Marie Butler-Knight*
Editorial Director: *Mike Sanders*
Senior Managing Editor: *Billy Fields*
Acquisitions Editor: *Michelle Wells*
Development Editor: *Ginny Bess Munroe*
Production Editor: *Kayla Dugger*

Copy Editor: *Michael Dietsch*
Cover Designer: *Bill Thomas*
Book Designer: *Trina Wurst*
Indexer: *Angie Bess*
Layout: *Chad Dressler*

Contents at a Glance

Contents

Introduction

My company's compensation expert drew me a graph showing a slow and steady ascent to retirement security. Consistent contributions to my 401(k) over the next 28 years would ensure a comfortable ride into post-employment bliss. It was this precise moment I decided there had to be a better way. Don't get me wrong—a comfortable retirement sure sounds better than a bankrupt one. But did I really have to sacrifice nearly three decades to reach the promised land? Also, would 50-hour workweeks and the occasional weekend in a cubicle be prerequisites for financial security?

I began to reverse my thinking. Instead of assuming my paycheck and 50-hour workweeks were givens in my life, I started from scratch. I asked myself how many hours I really wanted to work every week and the income I hoped to derive from those hours. My goal became to double my corporate America income while cutting my hours in half. In essence, I wanted to work three or four days per week while earning twice my paycheck.

Unfortunately, I had a feeling my boss wouldn't go for switching me to part-time while doubling my salary. Somehow I knew this wouldn't make good business sense. I was going to have to take charge of my career to truly work less and earn more.

Today, I'm proud to say I only work three or four days per week and my annual income is more than double my corporate America salary. I'm also proud to say I achieved this working-less, earning-more lifestyle without moving back in with my parents, borrowing money from an old roommate, bouncing a check, or meeting the repo man to take back my flat-screen TV. In other words, you can make significant changes in your career without suffering financial ruin.

Today, I derive my income from five major sources:

1. *Consulting:* Companies pay me a daily consulting rate to share with them the very skills and expertise I gained in my corporate job.

2. *Freelance writing:* Publishers, magazines, and online sites pay me to write articles and books on reaching your potential in career, love, and life.

3. *Coaching and public speaking:* People pay me to work with them personally to achieve their own career, love, and life goals and I also speak in front of audiences on personal development.

4. *Real estate income:* My wife and I own a two-family house near our primary residence that generates positive cash flow every month while our tenants continue to pay off our mortgage on the house.

5. *Internet marketing:* Thanks to cyberspace, people buy my audio CDs, books, and e-books while I sleep, play with my son, or go on dinner dates with my wife.

This transformation from corporate climber to consultant, writer, coach, speaker, real estate investor, and Internet marketer did not happen overnight. But it did take less than two years to redirect my ship. That's actually a pretty short time when you consider the alternative of 28 more years building a nest egg.

My goal in this book is to take you on the same journey toward working less and earning more. Whether you currently work in corporate America, run your own business, or can't find work at the moment, this is your chance to take charge of your own career and build a healthier balance of working versus leisure time.

In the *Complete Idiot's Guide to Working Less, Earning More*, I won't expect you to build the exact same revenue channels as me. Instead I'm going to coach you toward finding the path that best suits your income goals and unique skills. That might mean staying in your job but reshaping it, altering how you run your small business, building a consulting or freelance operation, or even generating passive income from real estate or Internet marketing. The point is you can change the working and earning givens in your life, and I'm going to show you precisely how to do it. So let's get started and leave the dinners at the office and missed baseball games with your kids to the people who don't read this book.

How This Book Is Organized

The chapters in this book are divided into three parts that take you on the journey toward working less and earning more.

Part 1, "Are You Overworked and Underpaid?" explains the downfall of the earn-and-burn approach and how to flip your script and become underworked and overpaid. You'll also learn the biggest fears that prevent people from changing their work situation as well as tangible steps to overcome those fears through outcome-focused goals.

Part 2, "Five Paths to Working Less and Earning More," breaks down five specific avenues you can take to build a working-less, earning-more lifestyle. These five approaches include reworking your current job, building a consulting practice, working freelance, running a business, and building passive income streams.

In **Part 3, "Integrating Personal Productivity and Financial Secrets into a 10-Year Success Program,"** you'll learn how outsourcing, organizational skills, and money management all play critical roles in both the time you spend working and the money you take home. We'll then put it all together to build your comprehensive program to lock in your working-less, earning-more lifestyle for the next decade and beyond.

Extras

Throughout this book, keep an eye out for little extras sprinkled into the margins. These sidebars include concrete suggestions, advice, and shortcuts to catapult you into the land of working less and earning more.

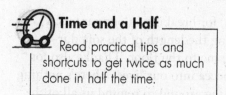

Time and a Half

Read practical tips and shortcuts to get twice as much done in half the time.

Ask Jeff

Learn solutions to the common questions about working less and earning more to gain from other people's experiences.

Less Is More

Learn to avoid the biggest energy wasters and pitfalls that can grind your new efficient self to a halt.

Fear Busters

See tangible tips and concrete guidance for overcoming the concerns that prevent people from making the changes necessary to work less and earn more.

Acknowledgments

Can one page really do justice to all the people who have helped you write a book? That's like asking an Academy Award winner to remember every producer, supporting actor, key grip, and hair stylist in two minutes or less. Still, I shall do my best to thank those most responsible for the pages in front of you before the orchestra plays me to commercial.

First and foremost, thank you to my wife, Carol, for rescuing me from a bachelor life filled with turkey clubs and Yankees games. Sure those World Series championships are satisfying, but my real adult life began the moment we met. You've taught me to live in the moment, reach beyond my capabilities, and truly become the man I was meant to be. Thanks also for those nine months of pregnancy and eighteen hours of labor that produced our son, Gabriel. I get winded carrying groceries in from the car; I can't imagine housing a human being all that time. Seeing you with Gabriel always wipes out the day's stress.

Thank you to my parents, Janis and Bert Cohen, for guiding me those first 25 years of my life. Everything I know about patience, being a good man, playing ping pong, earning good grades, traveling the world, building a loving family, and respecting your grandparents is attributable to you. Speaking of grandparents, thank you to Alice "Gram-Gram" Winitt for believing in my talents and telling me from the age of 12 I'd be a published author.

Thank you to my older sister, Alyssa, for breaking in our parents. I also accept your apology for stretching the length of the sofa during Saturday cartoons and relegating me to the floor. Thanks also for bringing Jeff #2, Samantha, and Rebecca into our lives. There's nothing like a couple of adorable nieces running around to remind us all of the importance of working less.

Thank you to Miriam, Victor, and Diana Mimon for welcoming me into your lives from day one. Miriam is my "Mommy #2" and treats me as "Son #1." Victor is the one who taught me to turn life's obstacles into stepping-stones. And Diana is the most creative, nurturing person I know. Thanks also to Daniel for loving Miriam and Jacqueline for loving Victor.

Thank you to Mark Levy for thinking about me for this book opportunity. Your innovative mind and compelling writing style continue to motivate me. Thanks to Janet Rosen and Sheree Bykofsky for championing this project from day one. You've been great sounding boards in navigating the world of publishing. Thanks also to Michele Wells, Kayla Dugger, Ginny Munroe, and the production team for guiding this book to market.

Finally, thank you to the wonderful mentors, colleagues, and friends who support me and my family in our working-less, earning-more lifestyle.

Trademarks

All terms mentioned in this book that are known to be or are suspected of being trademarks or service marks have been appropriately capitalized. Alpha Books and Penguin Group (USA) Inc. cannot attest to the accuracy of this information. Use of a term in this book should not be regarded as affecting the validity of any trademark or service mark.

Are You Overworked and Underpaid?

Given the choice of working more or working less, which would you choose? How about income? Would you like to make more or make less? Unless you're a glutton for long hours and little money, I'm guessing you'd prefer to work less and earn more. It makes you wonder why so many folks are overworked and under-paid when their goal is just the opposite.

In Part 1 of this book, we uncover why the rat race is synony-mous with working more and earning less. We then begin to lay out a road map for reversing the equation and helping you lead a truly balanced lifestyle. Finally, we examine the biggest obstacles that prevent people from changing their situation and how you can turn those obstacles into stepping-stones.

Chapter 1

Why Nobody Ever Wins the Rat Race

In This Chapter

- ◆ The risks of depending on long-term job security
- ◆ The difference between salary and what you actually take home
- ◆ How the rat race traps even the smartest mouse
- ◆ Prioritizing your life first, your job second
- ◆ Achieving a working-less, earning-more lifestyle

"Get a good education, land a quality job, work for 40 years, and build a nest egg for retirement." This is the basic American dream I was raised to believe. My dad followed this model and today his biggest worry is sinking a 7-foot putt to save double-bogey.

My experience, and that of many of my friends and colleagues, has been quite different. I spent eight years working at one large company. In that time I witnessed an end to employee pensions, a 15 percent workforce reduction, countless reorganizations, and one employee terminated just three years shy of retirement.

I survived the restructurings and layoffs but came away with three clear lessons. First, the only way to truly build a secure nest egg is to take charge of my own career. Second, working 40 to 60 hours per week under the illusion of job security is no way to make a living. Third, double-bogey is not a good golf score and my dad should consider woodworking or bird watching during his twilight years.

The Complete Idiot's Guide to Working Less, Earning More is all about changing your mindset. I switched from a typical corporate America job to working three or four days per week while more than doubling my corporate salary. This book will teach you to do the same without relying on lucky lottery numbers, suitcases full of cash inadvertently left in your trunk, or picking the right case on *Deal or No Deal*. Whether you work in corporate America, run your own business, or need to find work, this is your chance to build a lifestyle that truly balances income generation and leisure time. Yes, you can have it both ways, so let's get started on our journey toward working less and earning more.

A Brief Review of the Modern-Day Work Ethic

People seem to work all the time. Blame it on the BlackBerry, demanding bosses, the global economy, or your own belief that success is defined by total hours worked. All I know is we were not meant to answer e-mails in bed, conduct conference calls on transatlantic flights, or peck away on laptops during train commutes home. There was a time we read magazines in bed, watched movies on flights, and snoozed on trains. The line between work and leisure has been blurred, and many workaholics are letting their jobs completely define their life.

Don't get me wrong, there is nothing wrong with a strong work ethic. I just have to wonder whether the endgame payoff truly justifies the missed opportunities to watch *Breakfast at Tiffany's* while chomping on peanuts en route to Los Angeles. Is it possible the desire to earn more by working more is a flawed philosophy? Does working more necessarily guarantee a bigger financial payoff in the first place?

Ask Jeff

So what's wrong with burning the midnight oil to get ahead? I'm frequently asked this question by folks who find my three- or four-day workweek counterintuitive to earning more money. To them I say I never really found a direct correlation in the past between the hours worked and income earned. For example, in my corporate job I sometimes worked three or four weekends in a row to meet a deadline, but it had no positive effect on my salary that month.

If I had to guess, I'd say you're reading this book for one of five reasons:

◆ You work like a dog and are beginning to wonder whether the salary justifies the endless hours at the office.

◆ You've run some financials and realized your current salary does not have you on track for a comfortable retirement.

◆ You're interested in achieving a better work/life balance without sacrificing income or lowering your standard of living.

◆ You're unhappy at work and know you need to make some changes, but have no idea how to get started.

◆ Someone left this book on the train seat next to you and you prefer reading to staring at the back of a stranger's head.

For me, sitting in my corporate cubicle, the answer was all of the above (except for the last one because I hadn't written this book yet). I was working far too many hours, my comfortable retirement was a full 30 years away, I had a lousy work/life balance, and my gut told me some changes had to be made.

Less Is More

That little voice that tells you to make some changes in your life can be quite scary. Making changes feels so vague. Rather than paralyze your thinking in an endless cycle of worry, you've got to pinpoint why you want to change your situation. The more specific your thinking, the better your odds of making changes that directly improve what ails you. So get it all out on the table now and write down the top three reasons a change would do you good.

Today I earn zero salary from a corporate job. Instead, my income is earned through five main channels:

♦ Human-resources consulting for large corporations utilizing the expertise I gained during my tenure in corporate America.

♦ Freelance writing, including books, magazine stories, online articles, and blogs.

♦ Positive cash flow from a two-family house my wife and I purchased and rent out for more than our mortgage costs.

♦ Passive income from e-books, CDs, and traditional books sold through my website and online bookstores like Amazon.

♦ Speaking fees from seminars delivered on three main topics: career advancement, finding love, and personal development.

Let me save you the trouble and ask the questions I know are on your mind. How did a traditional corporate America guy become a consultant, writer, landlord, Internet marketer, and public speaker? How can a guy work less and earn more when it seems he now has five jobs instead of one?

I'd love to answer both questions right now, but then I'd have nothing left to write for the next 200+ pages. How about we make a deal? If you promise to keep reading, I'll promise five things in return:

♦ I'll lay out for you how I made my transition from corporate employee to what I do today.

♦ I'll break down how I make money through all five income channels and how you can do the same.

♦ I'll help you discover the right income channels to match your own expertise and passions.

♦ I'll prove to you that I earn more than double my corporate salary and I do it in three to four days per week.

♦ I'll free up so much time for you that you'll send me a letter asking me to write a follow-up book titled *The Complete Idiot's Guide to Doing Something When You Have Nothing to Do.*

I say take the deal. After all, you only have to make one promise to gain the benefit of five promises. That's a sweet deal if you ask me. So let me get started by explaining the difference between salary and success.

Why People Confuse Salary with Success

Here's a seemingly simple question for you. How much do you make? I'll bet a number flashed into your mind. With bonus and stock options or extra part-time work, the answer can fluctuate. But you probably have a pretty good idea what you earn each year. Or maybe you run a small business and income varies widely year to year. If that's the case, simply consider the average you made over the last three to five years.

Let's keep it simple and assume you make $100,000 per year. Most people never consider the work-related expenses that chip away at this six-figure salary. I'm a Virgo, which means I have good attention to detail. One of the benefits of this organized nature is I kept records of my spending during my corporate years. Following is a list of costs directly related to my job.

Work-Related Expenses That Chip Away at Your Salary

Expense Category	Annual Cost
Buying new suits or outfits	$500
Dry-cleaning the suits	$1,450
Fluff and fold laundry service	$1,150
Car fuel to and from train station	$1,800
Monthly pass to ride train to work	$2,500
Riding on subways to the office	$1,250
Parking/tolls when driving to office	$1,500
Breakfast from street vendors	$875
Lunches in the cafeteria	$3,100
Snacks from vending machines	$375
Happy hours with friends	$1,125
Dinner delivery after long day	$2,850
Total costs	$18,475

Time and a Half

There's an 11 in 12 chance you're not a Virgo and may not have detailed record keeping at your fingertips. That's okay; just pull out your last three credit-card bills. You can easily add up expenses related to your job. Multiply the total by four and you've got a reasonable estimate of yearly expenses. Throw in an extra cash estimate for those charges not on your credit card and you're good to go.

Holy guacamole, I'm spending nearly $20,000 annually on work-related expenses! On a $100,000-per-year salary, that's 20 percent of before-tax income on work expenses. Now this is the point where the critics emerge and make statements such as ...

♦ No matter how you make money, you'll still have to pay for new suits, dry cleaning, and laundry.

♦ Commuting is a fact of life, and changing jobs isn't necessarily going to cut your travel costs.

♦ We all need food to live, so breakfast, lunch, snacks, and dinner will still be part of the equation.

♦ You're treating your friends (and probably some strangers) too much at weekly happy hours.

I completely agree that you can't wipe out the entire $18,475 by changing jobs. However, allow me to address the four criticisms with my new reality:

♦ My work is predominantly from home, meaning less need for suits, less dry cleaning, and more time to do laundry myself.

♦ Commuting is not a fact of life when you work from home. There's no charge to walk from your bedroom to the home office.

♦ Three meals per day plus a snack is a great goal, but working from home lends itself to grocery shopping, which is cheaper.

♦ The funny thing about spending fewer days in an office is you don't go to happy hour quite as often.

I want you to take away one key message: your salary is not necessarily producing the income you might otherwise believe. The sooner you make this connection, the easier it becomes to consider alternative income streams. In other words, the salary you might be afraid to leave behind is not necessarily producing the desired money in your pocket.

Ask Jeff

When I break down work-related expenses for people, they often wonder why I focus on cutting expenses. After all, isn't the goal of this book to earn more? Absolutely, but one way to earn more is to spend less.

A New Vision: Learn to Pay Your Life First

Here's a challenge for you: randomly call five financial advisors and ask them for their number-one tip to save money and build a nest egg. I'll bet four out of five will recommend paying yourself first. The other advisor is on some island with that lone dentist who doesn't recommend Trident chewing gum.

Why do financial advisors recommend paying yourself first through automatic savings plans? Because they all know the deep, dark secret of consumers: if you give a consumer the chance to spend money instead of save it, he or she will choose the spending every time. That's because flat-screen televisions, trendy pocketbooks, and tickets to see U2 in concert are all so much sexier than transferring money to a mutual fund. Financial advisors know that if you automatically invest 10 percent of your income you'll lock in the savings before you pull up to the mall and blow that money on a $200 pair of designer jeans.

Investing $200 per month into a mutual fund instead of a pair of jeans may not seem like a big deal. However, thanks to compounding interest, $200 invested every month over 30 years with a 10 percent annual return becomes nearly $500,000. With half a million dollars on the line, you just might find a comfortable pair of jeans in your closet instead of the store.

Time and a Half

Here's a quick way you can calculate your own nest egg without an accounting degree. Go to FinishRich.com, a site run by David Bach, a premier financial advisor and educator. Go to his Latte Factor page, where you can calculate the savings you could accumulate by passing on that morning cup of Mocha Latte with extra whip. You'll quickly learn how small savings add up to big nest eggs.

How I Pay My Life First

A big breakthrough came for me when I realized automatic savings could be applied beyond just money management. The concept can extend to every aspect of your life. Every week contains exactly 168 hours. If you work in corporate America, then anywhere from 40 to 80 of those 168 hours are off the table. In other words, approximately 25 to 50 percent of your week is handed directly to your job (not to mention the additional 50 hours you plan to sleep every week). That's like buying those designer jeans before you consider saving the money instead.

My thinking reversed when I concluded those precious 168 hours should go to my life before my job, not the other way around. I want work to be the last thing on my to-do list, not the first. So here's how I started thinking about my 168 hours.

Jeff's Weekly To-Do List

Activity	Weekly Hours
Sleeping	55
Meals and snacks	20
Thinking big, dreaming, visioning	7
Free time with friends/family	30
Working out at the gym	4
Hobbies and new activities	5
Television, reading, Internet	10
Errands, bills, random to-do items	12
Working	25
Total hours	168

Notice work is last on my list. In fact, the activities are ranked from favorite to least favorite. I definitely enjoy sleeping, eating, and thinking big over errands, bills, random to-do items, and working. Most importantly, I'm paying my life first, not my job.

Now the math becomes simple. I only want to work 25 hours per week, roughly three days. Let's say I want to maintain a $100,000 income from my corporate America job. All I need to do is earn $80 per hour worked and my income remains the same. For those of us who did better in sociology than accounting, the calculation is as follows.

25 hours per week × $80 per hour = $2,000

$2,000 × 50 weeks worked per year = $100,000

I've even left two extra weeks for vacation, not that you'll need it after working only three days per week all year long. Don't worry, later in this book I'll outline exactly how to reach your per-hour target. So don't start fretting yet about who in this world will want to pay you $80 every time you offer up 60 minutes of your time. I know plenty of people. You will find them, too.

> **Less Is More**
>
> If you earn $100,000 today and you're working 50 hours per week, you're only earning $40 per hour. If you work 80 hours per week, then it drops to $25 per hour. Don't you owe it to yourself to cut those hours and raise your per-hour income? Why not get $80 or more per hour and rack up free time, not commuting time?

How You Can Pay Your Life First

You've seen a week in the life of your author, now how about you? Without worrying about how you'll make the money, fill in the following worksheet based solely on how you'd like to spend your time. I'll list the same categories plus some extras at the bottom for you to customize. If one of my categories is irrelevant for you, simply write zero hours in the space provided. The only requirement is to stop at 168 hours. If you know how to add extra hours in your week, I recommend writing *The Complete Idiot's Guide to Inventing an Eighth Day of the Week*. I guarantee it will be a best-seller.

My Weekly To-Do List

Activity	Weekly Hours
Sleeping	_____
Meals and snacks	_____
Thinking big, dreaming, visioning	_____
Free time with friends/family	_____
Working out at the gym	_____
Hobbies and new activities	_____
Television, reading, Internet	_____
Errands, bills, random to-do items	_____
Extra activity:_____	_____
Extra activity:_____	_____
Extra activity:_____	_____
Working	_____
Total hours	168

Now it's time to determine your hourly rate. All you need to do is divide your desired annual income (i.e., $100,000) by 50 (assuming you want to work 50 weeks per year), and then divide that number by the total hours you want to work each week (i.e., 25). In my example, $100,000 divided by 50 divided by 25 equals $80 per hour. Now it's your turn. Fill in the steps below and you'll arrive at the right hourly rate for you:

1. Write down your desired annual income: _____

2. Divide your desired annual income by 50: _____

3. Divide the number in step 2 by the total hours you plan to work each week: _____

The number you just wrote in step three represents your target hourly rate!

An hourly rate is just one way to reach your desired annual income. In this book, we consider daily consulting rates, real estate cash flow, passive income from Internet marketing, and even flat fees for freelance work. These all represent different avenues to reach your income target.

But I wanted to start with the hourly rate calculation to show you the simplest way of thinking about the money you need to earn each hour to maintain or raise your current income.

How to Set Outcome-Focused Goals

A goal without a desired outcome is like a ship with no rudder. Sure, you can float forever, but what's your destination? More importantly, how will you get there without steering? I had a goal to work less and earn more, but that's way too vague to be actionable. In fact, it's so vague you just might file it under "pipe dream" or "wishful thinking" rather than a potential reality. I knew that living a life based on working less and earning more would require outcome-focused goals. To highlight the difference between vague and outcome-focused goals, consider the following five goals:

- Stop working so many long hours before I suffer burnout.

- Consider consulting as an alternative income channel.

- Buy a rental property to generate monthly cash flow.

- Sell products online to make money while I sleep.

- Sign up for online freelance sites to supplement my income.

Here's what's wrong with these five goals. How will you know you've accomplished any of them? Would working one fewer hour each week mean you've stopped working so many long hours? Would buying the first rental property you see achieve your cash-flow target? You get the idea. Now let's turn these vague goals into action-oriented, outcome-focused goals.

- Reduce my weekly work hours from 50 to 25 and devote the freed-up time to working out, playing with my kids, and reading.

- Seek three consulting clients who are willing to pay me at least $640 per day so I can meet my $80-per-hour target.

- Buy a rental property where the cash flow from tenants is at least $1,000 higher than the mortgage and maintenance costs.

- Develop an e-book based on my expertise, sell it for $14.95 online, and sell at least 50 per week to generate $750 in passive income.

- Post my resumé on www.Guru.com and www.Elance.com but only apply for gigs that pay $80 per hour or a flat fee that roughly equates to the $80 per hour I'll spend on the project.

These five goals now pack quite a punch. Each is measurable, which means you'll know without a doubt whether you're on target. For example, when you see a potential rental property and realize it will generate $500 in monthly cash flow, you'll know to pass on it immediately. When a project on www.Guru.com sounds fun but only pays $25 per hour, you'll keep looking. However, when a consulting client wants to pay you $1,000 per day for your work, you'll jump at the opportunity.

The bottom line in working less and earning more is that saying "no" to the wrong work is equally as important as saying "yes" to the right opportunities. If you lock yourself into an underpaying consulting client just to make some money, you'll inadvertently make it impossible to reach your revenue targets. It took me some time to build the confidence to say "no" to the wrong work, but I've since learned that every "no" to Mr. Wrong Work opens the door for Mr. Right Work.

The Least You Need to Know

- Thanks to restructurings, layoffs, and reduced employee benefits, staying at one company is nowhere near the safe bet it used to be.

- Your annual salary is lower than you think due to work-related costs including dry cleaning, commuting costs, and meals at the cafeteria.

- The key to working less and earning more is to pay your life first by making work the last thing on your to-do list, not the first.

- You can calculate an hourly rate you need to be paid to reach your annual income and hours-worked goals.

- Writing a goal is meaningless unless you have a desired outcome associated with that goal.

2

How to Become Underworked and Overpaid

In This Chapter

♦ Finding the right balance of work and income

♦ Learning to work without sitting in a cubicle

♦ Choosing the right work for your personality type

♦ Losing your job without losing your shirt

Are you ready to officially enter the world of working less and earning more? I hope you're foaming at the mouth in anticipation of all the leisure time you can experience without sacrificing income. Actually, I hope you're not literally foaming because you might accidentally drench this book. Then the pages will stick together and you won't learn anything. Do us both a favor and grab a washcloth, napkin, or bib.

The transition to underworked and overpaid is not an overnight change. It takes foresight, planning, and even a little courage. The good news is you're about to acquire all the tools you need to make the transition as seamless as possible. From choosing your income and target work hours to finding the right work to suit your personality, this is the beginning of your journey. In this chapter, you also learn the importance of accepting transition assignments to bridge you from your job today to your ultimate work scenario.

For those of you who have worked solely in corporate jobs, I have good news and bad news. The good news is you may soon enter a world without bosses. The bad news is you may soon enter a world without bosses. You heard me right. You'll no longer have anyone telling you what to do, but while that can be a blessing, it also can be a curse. It's nice to not answer to anyone, but you'll also need to find the self-motivation to get things done without a supervisor laying out your deliverables for you. So let's get started on the path to making your working-less, earning-more lifestyle a reality.

Determining Your Desired Income and Hours You'll Work

It's time to put a stake in the ground. If we're going to make working less and earning more a reality, we need to define exactly what that means. How many hours do you really want to work each week, and how much income do you desire? We started working through these numbers in the previous chapter. Now it's time to make an official commitment. Fill in the blanks of the following two sentences:

I plan to work _____ hours each week.

I plan to earn _____ dollars each year.

Don't worry just yet about how you'll make these hours and income a reality. It's my job to get you there. For now, I just want you putting pen to paper to make a commitment to yourself. Without this information, how will we know when you're successful? I want you to someday rip out this page from your book and post it on the refrigerator like an A+ report card. You can even use cute magnets like farm animals, motivational sayings, or even a funny joke. Just don't rip out the page right now ... you'll miss what's written on the other side.

Ask Jeff

People often ask me how to choose the right targets for work hours and income. There's no right answer; this really is a personal decision. I started with the goal to cut my hours from 40 per week to 25 while maintaining my current income. Once I proved I could duplicate my income, I then sought to double my money while maintaining a 25-hour workweek.

Let's break down the hours-worked target even further. Suppose you want to work 25 hours each week. What's your plan? One choice would be to work from 9 A.M. Monday through 10 A.M. Tuesday. The plus side is you get six vacation days each week. The downside is you'll be so exhausted from your all-nighter you just might waste the next three days sleeping. The other end of the spectrum would be to target working seven days per week, approximately three to four hours each day. Here the advantage is you'll never work more than half a day. On the flip side, you'll never get a day off again. I went for the middle of the road ... working three to four days per week, anywhere from six to eight hours each day.

This is an important first question to answer because it will drive the kind of work to go for in your new life. I won't leave you hanging on this question, so here's a little quiz to help you out. Don't worry, unlike pop quizzes in high school there are no right or wrong answers here. For each question, circle the answer that best describes your preference.

Your Work Preference

Question #1: When do you tend to be most productive?

A) Morning

B) Afternoon

C) Evening

Question #2: How do you feel after working 8 to 10 hours straight?

A) Energized and ready for another 8 to 10 hours

B) Tired, but a nice meal afterward makes everything okay

C) Exhausted and likely to check the Internet for vacation deals

Question #3: Which of the following work scenarios sounds most appealing to you?

A) Working long hours two to three days per week with the payoff of four to five leisure days afterward

B) Working four to six hours per day, four or five days per week with the payoff of weekends and most evenings free

C) Working two to three hours per day, seven days a week with the payoff of extensive free time every single day

Question #4: Which kind of work environment feels most enticing to you?

A) Sitting in a home office predominantly by yourself

B) Working in an office setting with colleagues around you

C) Working "on-the-go" with appointments, travel, meetings, etc.

Question #5: Which kind of work feels most exciting to you?

A) Sitting at a computer to write or create spreadsheets

B) Working with your hands (i.e., carpentry, painting)

C) Meeting with people, presenting, or selling

You're probably expecting to add up your "A" answers, subtract your "B" answers, and divide by your "C" answers to discover you're meant to be a salesperson working 22.5 hours per week. Unfortunately, working less and earning more is not quite that scientific. In fact, it's okay if more than one answer appealed to you in a given question. Just use a bigger circle that covers two letters.

The idea is to use your answers to identify the best weekly hours structure for your personality. For example, maybe you're most productive in the morning, can't stand working more than four hours per day, love the isolation of a home office, and feel at ease with a computer. That's a completely different person from a night owl who can crank out 10 hours of solid work from midnight to morning, and prefers meeting with others over the loneliness of a home office.

Less Is More

Keep in mind that the fewer hours you'll be working each week the more important it is to be productive during those hours. In a 40-hour workweek, it may be okay to slack off for 5 to 10 hours each week. That luxury is gone in the shortened workweek. So you'll want to really identify when you're most productive to get the most bang for your buck.

Your goal here is to identify themes from the quiz that can help you determine how to structure your week. For example, let's say I answered "C" to all five questions. What does that say about me?

♦ Clearly I prefer working at night.

♦ Long stretches of uninterrupted work are not my thing.

♦ I'd work every day if it meant ample daily free time.

♦ I'm an "on-the-go" type, not a "behind-the-desk" type.

♦ I'm a people person, not a work-on-my-own type.

You can tell right away that working in isolation for long stretches would not be the way to go. What about you? List five insights you found from your quiz answers.

Your Insights

Insight #1: _____

_____

Insight #2: _____

_____

Insight #3: _____

_____

Insight #4: _____

_____

Insight #5: _____

_____

Now put these five insights into one sentence that captures how best to structure your workweek. In my example where I answered "C" for all five questions, my sentence might read:

> I want to work in the evenings for no more than three or four hours per day, with most of the work outside the house interacting with people.

Now it's your turn. Write one sentence to sum up how best to structure your hours.

Your Sentence:

_____

_____

_____

_____

 Fear Busters

What if the sentence you just wrote sounds nothing like your current work scenario? Let's say you currently work 9 to 5 in an office and your ideal setup is mornings only, seven days per week? Don't worry, the rest of this book will show you exactly how to make the transition. So don't get scared—get excited by the possibilities.

We are off and running. We've got your working hours and income targets written down. We also know what kind of work structure best suits your personality. Now it's time for a little lesson in getting work done without a cubicle to box you in.

Learning to Get Work Done Without the Need for a Cubicle

I spent eight years in a cubicle. Actually, I earned an office for the last three years, but I felt like I was in a fishbowl. It was like living in an aquarium with people peering in to see me. I expected fish food to be tossed in my office at lunchtime. Instead I devoured a steady diet of turkey club sandwiches and the panini of the day. In case you haven't guessed by now, cubicle and office life is not for me.

I must admit, however, that cubicles and offices do serve one important purpose. Both are constant reminders that it's time for work, not play. Just like your bed is an indicator of sleep and the kitchen is an indicator of mealtime, your cubicle or office reminds you to get stuff done (by the way, just to whet your appetite, a whole section on productivity awaits you later in this book).

Living a life of freedom from the office is both a blessing and a curse. As much as we may dislike our bosses telling us what to do, life is easier when someone else guides you. It's similar to a health club where your workout is better with a personal trainer guiding you rather than relying on self-motivation. I must admit it took a good three to six months before I successfully learned how to manage my own day. I'm not proud of that timeline, but it's better than giving up and crawling back to a typical corporate job. Allow me to shave months off your timeline by giving you a before-and-after look at my typical day. Keep in mind I went from sitting in a corporate office five days per week to working predominantly from home.

Jeff's Day Before He Learned Self-Motivation

Do you remember your last sick day from work? You sat home with the sniffles, resting in your pajamas, and waiting for chicken soup to be delivered by a caring friend or family member. You probably also noticed that being home on a Tuesday has some advantages, like random household to-do items creeping into your day (although some folks might consider that a disadvantage).

- You can catch up on your favorite game shows, soap operas, and on-demand movies.

- You can spend hours surfing the Internet, e-mailing friends, and watching humorous bits on YouTube.

- You can have a contractor over to your house to fix a leaking pipe, install a new appliance, or deliver a sofa.

- You can reorganize a closet, start a scrapbook, or cook a brand-new recipe for crispy chicken with red peppers.

Ask Jeff _____

I don't blame you if you're thinking right now that TV, Internet surfing, laughing at YouTube, installing appliances, and starting scrapbooks are worthy pursuits. I agree, mindless entertainment, home improvement, and fun projects all have their place. The point is that these little tasks have a way of consuming your day if you're not careful. With the limited hours you'll be working in your new life, you need to guard against this potential pitfall.

The bottom line is your home is a place of comfort but also a huge distraction. Every day can feel like a sick day if you're not careful, and that's a bad way to be productive. Here's a snapshot of my typical day before I got a handle on self-motivation and took charge of my working time.

Jeff's Typical Day Before Self-Motivation

Time	Activity
7–9 A.M.	Wake up somewhere in this two-hour range.
9–10 A.M.	Enjoy cereal or eggs (if willing to cook).
10 A.M.–noon	Surf the net for news and catch up on e-mails.
Noon–2 P.M.	Have lunch and then begin work for the day.
2–4 P.M.	Work interrupted by delivery, contractor, doctor appointment, or other distraction.
4–6 P.M.	Get back to work.
6–7 P.M.	Pick up my wife at train station.
7–9 P.M.	Enjoy dinner together, catch up on our days.
9–10 P.M.	Watch TV together or read magazines.
10–11 P.M.	Wind down for bedtime.

Allow me to share three key facts from my working life before I learned self-motivation:

♦ I knew more about current events than a CNN anchor.

♦ The house never looked cleaner or more organized.

♦ I only managed to work about 2 or 3 hours per day even though I was home alone for 10 to 12 hours total.

Maybe my ultimate goal is to work 2 hours per day, but I don't need to allot 10 to 12 to make that goal. The idea is to compartmentalize your time so you control your working hours. Slowly but surely I reorganized my day to take control of my working time and self-motivate to get things done.

Jeff's Day After He Learned Self-Motivation

After three to six months of trial and error, I finally got a hang of how to structure my days. Here's the new look. Compare it to my previous day and notice the differences.

Jeff's Typical Day with Self-Motivation

Time	Activity
7–9 A.M.	Set alarm for 7 A.M., review to-do list for day.
9–10 A.M.	Scan e-mails for anything urgent.
10 A.M.–noon	Shut down Internet and get to work.
Noon–2 P.M.	Have lunch and then continue working.
2–4 P.M.	Continue working.
4–6 P.M.	Work interrupted by delivery, contractor, doctor appointment, or other distraction.
6–7 P.M.	Pick up my wife at train station.
7–9 P.M.	Enjoy dinner together, catch up on our days.
9–10 P.M.	Watch television together or read magazines.
10–11 P.M.	Wind down for bedtime.

Allow me to share three key facts from my working life after I learned self-motivation:

- ◆ I wrote to-do lists at the beginning of each week and reviewed them to start my working day to guide exactly what needed to be accomplished that day.

- ◆ I managed to work six uninterrupted hours.

- ◆ I still stayed on top of the latest news without devoting two hours per day to Internet surfing.

Less Is More _____

I know we live in an age of multitasking. We believe that conducting conference calls, checking e-mails, and working on a presentation all at the same time makes us superhuman. In my experience, it has the opposite effect. We don't pay attention on the call, send e-mails with spelling mistakes, and craft presentations lacking our full attention and creativity. Working less goes best with focusing on one thing at a time and doing it faster.

Ten Tips to Help You Take Charge of Your Day

You've seen my life before and after I learned to control my time. This really is critical in a world where you want to get everything done in half the time, especially if you'll be working from home. Your day will of course vary depending on how you chose to structure it in the previous section. Still, here are 10 universal tips that can help you control your time, avoid distractions, and get done what needs to get done. Master these tips and by all means use your extra free time to start that scrapbook, install a new washer/dryer, or clean out your closet to find that long-lost pair of your favorite designer blue jeans.

1. **The Internet.** Shut down the Internet when you don't need it. I can be working on a presentation and for some reason I'll click over to a sports site to check the injury report on my fantasy football squad. A simple act like closing the Internet can eliminate this enticing distraction.

2. **The Phone.** Let unexpected and nonurgent calls go to voicemail. Answering the phone can lead to a five-minute conversation or a two-hour discussion. You don't always know what you'll get, so let your answering machine take a message and get back to work.

3. **The Maintenance People.** Limit deliveries, installations, and other house calls to set times each week. When you're home all day, it's easy to offer 9 to 5 for people to come to your house. Just because you're physically in your house does not mean you need to be available the entire time.

4. **The Television.** Store your television clicker in the television stand cabinet. You take a break from work, microwave a turkey enchilada, and sit on the couch to devour your meal. You notice the clicker by your side and pretty soon you're engrossed in an after-school special. Leave the remote in the cabinet and you'll be less likely to turn the television on in the first place.

5. **The To-Do Lists.** Make monthly, weekly, and daily to-do lists. Work rarely gets done when you choose your to-do items based on mood or spontaneity. Write down those marching orders and take them seriously.

6. **The Office Space.** Respect your home office as a place of business. The nanny pops in with a question about baby food. Your wife comes home mid-day for a lunch break. The idea is not to cut yourself off from the outside world, but you do need some boundaries to make sure your working time is really your working time.

7. **The Snail Mail.** Pick up mail at the end of the day. You hear the mailman's footsteps and like a trained puppy you march to the door. It's mostly junk mail, but you can't help opening the envelopes and paying a bill or two. This five-minute diversion can easily turn into 60 minutes.

8. **The Small Tasks.** Delegate nonrevenue-generating activities. There are lots of tasks people are willing to do for anywhere from $5 to $15 per hour. Examples might include cleaning your house, doing laundry, or balancing the books. Sure this expense comes off your bottom line, but it might be worth focusing on earning $100 or more in that hour instead of folding socks and underwear.

 Time and a Half

Let's say you need to wash four loads of laundry and work on a client presentation. Both need to get done today because there is not a clean towel to be found in the house, the kids have nothing to wear to school tomorrow, you're out of clean shirts, and the presentation is due tomorrow. You're only one person, but you can get both things done by delegating the nonrevenue-generating activity. Look for areas of your life that can be outsourced inexpensively and instead focus your limited time on generating income to reach your goal.

9. **The IMs.** Avoid the temptation of instant messaging. You're cruising through a project on your computer when all of a sudden your screen is hijacked by a message from your old college roommate. "Whatcha up to tonight?" says the message innocently enough. It's okay to say you're busy at the moment and will call him later to make plans. Better yet, shut off the IM feature when you're deep into work.

10. **The Progress Checks.** Take a moment to check in with yourself during the day. If I'm planning to work six hours in a given day, I'll check in on my progress halfway through. I'll look at my to-do list to see whether the most important to-do's are on track. If not, I'll reshuffle the rest of my day to get the right work done.

Finding the Right Work Scenario for Your Vision and Goals

You've got the hours you want to work, you've got the revenue target, and you even have a sense of how to schedule out your weekly hours to match your personality and productivity tendencies. One big question still remains. How exactly will you earn your money? It's not enough to just book five hours for work on Mondays, Wednesdays, and Fridays. You need a game plan for rolling in the dough.

Part 2 of this book lays out five specific paths to creating a working-less, earning-more lifestyle:

- ◆ Changing the nature of your current job

- ◆ Becoming a consultant

- ◆ Working freelance

- ◆ Running a business

- ◆ Generating passive income

I've actually incorporated all five strategies into my own approach. Other successful work-less, earn-more people I know have focused solely on one of the five strategies. Either way can work. Which one is right for you depends on whether you prefer to play chess or race cars.

I know what you're thinking: What do chess and race cars have to do with working less and earning more? Allow me to explain.

The Chess Model

In chess, you systematically move your pieces forward. You can't win by playing solely with one pawn or just the queen. It takes a concerted team effort to win. So you slowly move your pieces toward your opponent in an organized fashion. A few chess pieces are your explorers while others play defense. But every piece has a role; every piece works toward your common goal of checkmate.

The chess model is most similar to the approach I took in working less and earning more. I initially generated income by changing my corporate job to a work-from-home, part-time gig. I then began earning money through consulting and freelance writing. I packaged up my services into a small business. Finally, the passive income started rolling in through real estate investments, as well as e-books and CDs I sold through a website. These revenue channels can be thought of as chess pieces. They work together to reach my goal of working less and earning more. Notice I'm not betting on one particular approach. My revenue channels are like a diversified portfolio of stock investments. If one or two earn money, it makes up for the others falling behind.

> **Less Is More**
>
> You might be wondering how consulting, freelance writing, running a small business, and earning passive income could possibly take less time than a straightforward corporate job. It seems like four jobs instead of one. But I found that doing my own thing cuts out bureaucracy, office politics, and incessant team meetings. Instead I cut right to the chase and do what needs to be done.

The Race Car Model

Here's a question. If you were a famous NASCAR driver, how many cars would you enter in a race? The answer is one. You get behind the wheel of one race car, ride it as fast as possible, and hope for the best. There's no backup plan, there's no second car to help win the race if the first car falters. You're putting all your eggs in the performance of one car.

Similarly, in working less and earning more, you could choose to bet on one revenue channel. Rather than systematically moving chess pieces forward, it's like picking one chess piece and hoping for the best.

Comparing race cars to working less and earning more, this would be like choosing one revenue channel, say consulting, and pouring all your energy into it. There's one key advantage and one disadvantage to the race car model as compared to the chess model:

♦ **Advantage of the race car model:** Many an entrepreneur will tell you the key to business success is laserlike focus and distraction avoidance. You figure out how to make money, funnel your energy into this income channel, and avoid superfluous activities that contribute little to the bottom line. If you ran a bakery that sold donuts and muffins and the donuts outsold the muffins five to one, you wouldn't waste precious hours concocting new muffin recipes. You'd focus all your energy on baking, marketing, and selling donuts to the masses. In essence, you're squeezing every last drop of income out of your best idea instead of making some money from multiple good or average ideas.

♦ **Disadvantage of the race car model:** What if investing time in new muffin recipes could lead to a new taste that becomes a customer sensation? You focused solely on donuts, made a reasonable income, but ignored what could have become your cash cow. The race car model does not allow for dabbling in multiple income streams to see which takes off. If you're trying to earn $100,000, then you're working with a nondiverse portfolio where your one idea needs to generate the full $100,000. If you went with the chess model instead, you could earn $20,000 or $25,000 from each of four or five good ideas. Then if one idea has a down year, you potentially can make it up through one of your alternative income streams.

Ask Jeff

So should you be a chess master or a race car driver? Why not take the hybrid approach? Begin your work-less, earn-more journey as a chess player and dabble in four or five revenue channels. See which one or two catch on fastest. Then convert into a race car driver and funnel your energies into the best idea. But keep that chessboard handy so you can fall back on alternative income channels if your best idea falters.

Whether you go with the chess model or race car approach, the next obvious question is how to really make your money. Let's break down five approaches to working less and earning more. I know this will whet your appetite for the full chapters on each approach coming your way in Part 2.

Changing the Nature of Your Current Job

As you may have realized by now, over the course of my corporate career I developed a severe allergy to cubicles and offices. I just knew a lifetime in corporate America was not for me. Many a night I dreamed of storming into my supervisor's office, knocking the paperwork off his desk, spilling coffee on his lap, deleting his e-mail inbox, and flushing his BlackBerry down the toilet. I'd then announce "I quit" in a triumphant moment and storm out as an orchestra played "Take This Job and Shove It."

Okay, so maybe the dream wasn't quite so vivid, but you get the idea. I wanted a new life that didn't revolve around team meetings, watercooler chat, incessant e-mails and voicemails, and more red tape than a gift-wrapping department during the holiday season.

One word stopped me from playing out my fantasy. That word is "money." Quitting would be dramatic, but it wouldn't pay the rent or put food on the table. Still, you can create a working-less, earning-more lifestyle without quitting your job. In Chapter 4, we discuss the virtual office, compressed workweek, and extended vacation as three ways to build the life you want without giving up the steady paycheck.

Becoming a Consultant

Every day you work in corporate America, you pick up valuable skills to add to your personal toolbox. You might be learning analytical tools, presentation skills, sales techniques, accounting formulas, or even technology solutions. The problem with a corporate job is you don't necessarily make the connection between getting paid and displaying these skills. Instead you believe you're earning a paycheck in exchange for showing up at the office. You're also not spending your entire day showing off these skills. Instead much of your day is filled up with meetings, responding to requests, clearing out e-mails, and chatting up co-workers.

> **Time and a Half**
>
> The best part about consulting is you can double dip on income generation. Let's say you're delivering a sales training course to a Fortune 500 company. You'll get paid for your time, of course. But you also can sell a training manual, book, or personal coaching as an add-on product/service. Now you're making twice the income in half the time.

As a consultant, the connection between your skill set and income is crystal clear. You get paid for every hour or day you share your skills with a client. If you're a change-management consultant, you get paid when you roll out a change-management plan and implement it for a client. If you're a sales consultant, you might get paid for creating and facilitating a sales training class for an organization. If you are an architect, you get paid after designing that new kitchen layout. In Chapter 5, you learn how to create your own consulting firm based around the unique skills you've gathered from your work experiences.

Working Freelance

Working freelance sounds exotic to many corporate climbers. Maybe it's the word "free" that makes it sound so unstructured. Since leaving my corporate job, I've earned freelance income from writing magazine articles, crafting blogs for websites, coaching job seekers on resumé and cover-letter writing, and even creating PowerPoint slides and talking points for busy corporate executives presenting to the board of directors. You might think magazines, blogs, resumés, and PowerPoint have very little in common. In fact, all four made use of my skills and background in human resources and personal development. They were just different channels for me to share my knowledge and expertise with the world.

In Chapter 6, you learn how to build a base of loyal, high-paying freelance clients who can make your working-less, earning-more dreams a reality. From building power relationships to generating profitable online leads, and leveraging industry associations, you'll get equipped with everything it takes to score more freedom from freelance gigs.

Running a Business

You've heard the stories ... a guy works 120 hours per week for five years before finally making it big and selling the business or taking it public for millions. There's nothing wrong with this aspiration. Just ask the founders of Google, MySpace, or Microsoft.

This model runs counter to working less and earning more because you'll be working more than ever before in the hopes of hitting the jackpot. In Chapter 7, I help you break the mentality that the only way to make money in a small business is to let it infiltrate every fiber of your life. You learn the power of delegation and outsourcing, how to find the cash cows in your business model, and when to take on partners to balance the workload.

Generating Passive Income

Why should being awake be a prerequisite for making money? Thanks to real estate investing, Internet marketing, and royalty payments, you can count sheep while the bank counts your money. Since transitioning to a working-less, earning-more lifestyle, I actually make money from all three channels. I own a two-family home that generates positive cash flow through rental income. I sell e-books and CDs online to spread my message about reaching your potential in career, love, and life. I also earn royalty payments from the books I write.

Similar to the chess versus race car model, you can decide if all three or just one of these passive income channels is right for you. In Chapter 6, I provide more detail on all three. Notice this chapter is not about buying zero-down foreclosures, get-rich-quick Internet secrets, or pyramid schemes. Chapter 6 is all about the nuts and bolts of creating realistic passive income channels that can keep the cash flowing day and night.

Transition Assignments to Bridge You to the Work You Desire

I wish I could tell you I quit my job on a Monday and by Tuesday morning I had accomplished the following:

- Set up a consulting business to capitalize on the unique skills and talents gained in corporate America

- Scored five freelance clients to generate a steady stream of fun and exciting projects I could complete on my own time

- Purchased a two-family home, found tenants, and started earning positive cash flow from the rental income

- Launched my small business and made *Fast Company*'s annual list of the fastest-growing companies in America

- Designed a website and attracted millions of e-book and CD-buying customers who helped me earn money while I hit the treadmill, watched DVDs, or dozed in a rocking chair

The reality is that it took some time to set up these revenue channels and set them up right. I stumbled, I made mistakes, and I course-corrected along the way. But I kept my goal of working less and earning more front and center along the way. I also kept those fears of failure at bay to give myself the best possible shot at success. The next chapter will cover all the reasons people fail to go for it and how to overcome these obstacles and turn them into stepping-stones.

 Fear Busters

> Is it really worth risking your cozy corporate job for a shot at working less and earning more? Flash ahead 30 years and assume you stayed in your current job the entire time. Would the comfortable nest egg justify the years given to your company? If so, then maybe there's no need to shake things up. But if there's any chance you'll feel a lifetime of regret, then it's time to take action.

I'm not a risk taker by nature. The thought of going from a six-figure income to zero did not sound appealing to me. I'd actually prefer a root canal over building back to that income from scratch. That's where a transition assignment is your ticket to working less and earning more without risking everything. I negotiated a three-day-per-week, work-from-home arrangement with my company for a period of three months. After that stretch, I signed a six-month consulting project with my company to basically perform my old responsibilities while they searched for my permanent replacement.

To help quash your own fears of giving up that cozy job for a shot at working less and earning more, here are six transition options you could choose to bridge you from your current situation to your dream scenario.

Choice 1: Switch to Part-Time

Remember, the goal isn't to switch to working less and earning more overnight. The idea is to systematically migrate to this lifestyle. A part-time gig accomplishes two things simultaneously.

First, you keep a percentage of your current income. Okay, so maybe you'll have to cut back on fancy restaurant dinners and exotic travel. But at least your lights will be on, the heat will be cranking, and you won't get evicted. Second, you'll experience extra free days each week to make your game plan. It's amazing how four free days each week instead of two frees your mind to think big.

Choice 2: Negotiate a Consulting Gig

Leaving your job creates an immediate sense of urgency for your employer. Where will they ever find someone like you to accomplish all the wonderful things you got done day to day? The answer is you. It's a win-win for you and your company to negotiate a temporary consulting assignment while your company searches for your replacement. Who knows your job better than you? Who is in a better position to train your replacement than you?

The answers to these two questions are nobody and nobody. You may think your company will want no part of you after you announce your intentions to leave. It's true this might be the initial emotional reaction. Then business needs will kick in and your company will realize the many benefits of keeping you on the books for a transition period.

Choice 3: Start Freelancing at Night

Who says you have to quit your job before accepting your first free-lance assignment? Granted, your company may have rules against earning secondary income while under their employment. So check with Human Resources before you get yourself in hot water. Assuming your company doesn't block secondary sources of income, you can absolutely build this revenue channel before flushing your supervisor's BlackBerry.

There are three great ways to attract freelance clients. These include networking, freelance websites, and industry associations. We cover all three in depth in Chapter 6; I've used all three to build a stable of paying freelance customers. For now, just know you can make new friends, surf freelance sites, and join a new association before you give your two-week's notice.

Ask Jeff

Choices are a blessing and a source of confusion. Here we have six ways you could bridge yourself to working less and earning more. But which one is right for you? It's like getting offered six delicious desserts and not knowing where to sink your spoon. There is no right answer. In fact, I incorporated multiple choices to build the confidence necessary to make the transition.

Choice 4: Outsource Website Design

If you're going the Internet marketing route, you'll need a website. I initially wanted to learn the nuts and bolts of website design and under-took the project myself. I quickly realized it would take months to get up to speed on JavaScript, shopping carts, newsletters, and hyperlinks. Rather than learn a foreign language, I began a search for qualified website designers.

To my surprise, building a website does not require taking out a second mortgage on your house. In fact, sites abound where you can post your website project and people will bid to win your business. A funny thing happens when multiple people bid on the same business—it drives the price down and the quality up. That's good news for you as the consumer. My early sites were built for $300 or less and I was up and running in less than a month. For that price and timeframe I'll gladly leave JavaScript and hyperlinks to the professionals.

Choice 5: Buy a Rental Property Now

Who says you have to quit your job to purchase a cash-flow-generating rental property? In fact, Sunday is the most popular day for open houses. So if you're eager to get a jump on real estate investing, keep your job for now and chase open-house signs after Sunday brunch. By the way, showing steady corporate income just might make landing a good mortgage easier versus the uncertainty of business start-up income.

In Chapter 8, we'll break down how to find the right property. For now, just keep these five rules of thumb in mind and you'll be headed in the right direction:

- Look at rentals in your target neighborhood to get a sense of realistic prices you can charge for tenants.

- Keep in mind the amenities that attract tenants, including washer/dryer, central air, good schools, and proximity to mass transportation.

- Remember the costs that will take away from your cash flow, including lawn care, house maintenance, and unexpected damage or broken appliances.

- When you calculate cash flow, assume your property will be vacant three months every year. You might get lucky and sign a great tenant to a long-term lease. But you also might experience gaps between when one tenant leaves and the next signs.

- Know the difference between friendship and a business. It's tempting to become friends with your tenants. But friends ask for extensions when they owe you money. The last thing you want is a tenant saying "I'll gladly pay you double the rent next month for a free month today."

Choice 6: Cut a Deal with Your Spouse

My wife and I went on the working-less, earning-more journey together. At the time, we both worked in corporate America. One of the ways we mitigated our risk was to decide one of us would go for it while the other kept their day job. I guess I won the coin flip, because my wife agreed to stay at work while I built our new life.

This option may not exist for you if you're single or your spouse doesn't earn enough to support you. But it's a great option if the numbers make sense and your spouse is supportive. Be sure to throw in some foot rubs and gift certificates to your spouse's favorite stores to sweeten the deal.

The Least You Need to Know

- ◆ To reach your desired working and earning goals, you need to begin by setting targets.

- ◆ Working less and earning more requires a transition from the boss telling you what to do to self-motivation.

- ◆ One of the most important steps in working less and earning more is to choose the right work for your personality, skills, and passions.

- ◆ Seeking transition assignments to bridge you from your job today to your dream work situation takes the immediate pressure off paying your bills.

Chapter 3

3

Turning Obstacles into Stepping-Stones

In This Chapter

◆ The top reasons that prevent people from going after a working-less, earning-more lifestyle

◆ Real-life solutions to overcoming your fears and going for it

◆ The importance of building a powerful network that can guide and help you make the transition

◆ Taking those first small steps to generate the momentum you'll need to be successful

Who is going to win ... you or that little voice in your head that says don't do it? You're at a crossroads right now. You can continue reading this book passively or spring into action and truly build a working-less, earning-more life. I can give you the tools, I can share my experiences, and I can even send you an e-mail of encouragement.

What I can't do is make this happen for you. But I can do the next best thing. I can bring up all the fears, negativity, and what-if scenarios that could stop you in your tracks. I know this list by heart because everything you're about to read almost derailed my own efforts. Nobody is immune from anxiety, and nobody can guarantee with 100 percent certainty your efforts will work out. I will, however, list all of the reasons that scare people from going for it and give you the encouragement and tools to wipe away those fears and conquer your demons.

In this chapter, we cover the top reasons people let anxiety and unfounded fears win, as well as concrete tips for overcoming these challenges. You also learn how building a powerful network of mentors, guides, and subject matter experts can help you transition exponentially faster to a working-less, earning-more lifestyle. Finally, you read about ways to generate early momentum and build the confidence to make your dream work scenario a reality. So let's leave all the scary stuff to the horror movies and conquer our fears together.

The Top Reasons People Fail to Change Their Situations

Which of the following statements do you believe best represents my earliest thinking when I contemplated leaving corporate America to work less and earn more?

- I'll double my salary in less than a month and make my old co-workers jealous.

- I haven't made a decision this smart since investing a few dollars in Google before the big IPO.

- It might take a few months, but sooner or later I'll hit my stride and prove the doubters wrong.

- This might be a bigger mistake than eating Oreo cookies and gummy bears before a dentist appointment.

I'll tell you right now that bullet points one and two never crossed my mind. I'll also tell you I wish bullet three dominated my thinking, but that's not true. My initial beliefs centered around one common thought … this could be a huge mistake!

Why would I share my doubts and fears with you, the reader? Well, it's nice to look back fondly now at the self-inflicted obstacles that almost stopped my journey before it started. More importantly, I want you to know it's normal to lack self-confidence at the beginning of an ambiguous ride. In fact, I'll bet you could list five reasons right now to stick it out in your current situation rather than risk a change. I'll bet you could crank out that list in under a minute, too. Let's test that theory. Right here, right now, list the first five reasons that pop into your head telling you not to go for it. Ready, set, write.

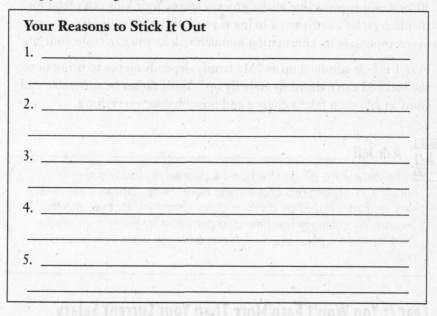

Your Reasons to Stick It Out

1. _____

   _____

2. _____

   _____

3. _____

   _____

4. _____

   _____

5. _____

   _____

I may not be a mind reader, but I'm pretty sure I could guess at least three of the reasons on your list. Let's test that theory, too. Here is what I consider the top 10 reasons people fail to change their situation. If I manage to guess all five, please submit a letter to my editor requesting that for my next book I write *The Complete Idiot's Guide to ESP*.

By the way, in the next section I'll teach you exactly how to conquer each of the 10 fears. I faced all 10, beat all 10, and that cleared my mind and emotions to really go for the life I imagined. That's why I want you to face your own fears right now and turn those obstacles into stepping-stones.

Fear 1: You Won't Be Able to Support Your Family

When you're single, you only have yourself to blame if a new venture goes belly up. When you're married, the pressure increases because your soul mate's future is jointly riding on your decisions. But nothing compares to that first child entering your life. You look at this defenseless child that can't walk, talk, or even feed itself and suddenly all risk-taking melts away quicker than an ice cream cone next to a bonfire.

Consider my wife, for example. Before she met me she would go sky-diving, bungee jumping, and motorcycle riding. Now we have a baby at home. The riskiest thing I've seen her do is sneak 11 items into the 10-or-fewer express line at the grocery store. Your kids can't fend for themselves, let alone earn a living if you fall flat on your face. So you overcompensate by eliminating as much risk as you can from your life.

Fear 1 is best summed up as "My family depends on me to bring home the bacon; I can't afford to go belly up." You'd rather be miserable and comfortable than take a chance and possibly lose everything.

Ask Jeff

People ask me all the time how I supported my family during the transition to working less and earning more. Three steps took the pressure off. First, I stayed on part-time at my current job for three months. Second, my company hired me as a consultant for the next six months. Third, my wife agreed to stay in a corporate job while I charted my own path.

Fear 2: You Won't Earn More Than Your Current Salary

I worked in corporate America for eight years. The average annual salary increase was 4 percent. Some years I earned 8 percent, other years only 3 percent. After a while you recognize the trend and can anticipate your future salary 5 or 10 years from now.

Once your mind locks in on the expected salary increases, it can be difficult to imagine doubling or tripling your income. It seems out of the ordinary, unlikely, and therefore not worth considering. There's this weird comfort zone that comes from knowing what to expect even if you could do better.

Fear 2 is best described as "My company is willing to pay me $X per year for my efforts. Why would someone else pay me double?" You just can't visualize that your skills could net more money than what someone is currently paying you.

Fear 3: You Don't Deserve to Work Less and Earn More

Picture this scenario. It's Tuesday morning around 10:45 A.M. You're walking downtown with a tennis racket, decked out in a dark blue jump suit and shiny white sneakers. In 15 minutes you'll be meeting your tennis instructor for a one-hour lesson. Men and women in dark dress suits whisk by you on the way to business meetings. Which statement best describes your mindset:

- ◆ I should probably get back to work myself; a morning tennis lesson feels like I'm playing hooky from the office.

- ◆ These businessmen and women have it all wrong. Life is about morning tennis lessons, not trudging to another meeting.

Fear 3 is all about the first bullet. "Weekdays are for working, not playing. If I'm holding a tennis racket on Tuesday morning instead of a BlackBerry, I'm cheating the system." You just don't believe you deserve to earn your income in less time. Everyone else is putting in 40-hour workweeks; you should, too.

Fear 4: You're Not Smart Enough to Pull It Off

Have you ever walked into a Starbucks on the way to work and seen a guy in jeans pecking away at his laptop? You can't help but wonder what job lends itself to casual dress and carefree computer typing. Why are you chugging café lattes on the way to mindless team meetings while this guy lounges in a cozy coffeehouse?

Sure you can dismiss Mr. Starbucks as a starving artist. But you just might wonder if he somehow cracked the code on earning a living without all the stress, deadlines, and pressure.

Fear 4 boils down to "I just can't picture how to go from a guy in a suit to a guy in a Starbucks." You believe he must be smarter, luckier, or more experienced than you. Otherwise he never would have pulled off this seemingly attractive lifestyle.

Time and a Half _____

Rather than wondering forever what that guy at Starbucks does for a living, why not muster the courage to ask him? One time I busted out of my shy shell and inquired what a stranger was writing on his laptop. Turns out he was a consultant in the same field as me and we ended up working jointly on a future project. Innocent questions can lead to big bucks in no time.

Fear 5: You Were Raised to Believe in a Steady Paycheck

Your dad worked 30 years at one company. His loyalty was rewarded with a generous pension, benefits for life, and a comfortable retirement nest egg. Today his time is equally divided between the driving range and drive-in movies.

When you talk to your dad about giving up the steady paycheck, he points to himself as proof positive that company loyalty equals safety and security. Why live in the land of the unknown when you can stay in your job and know you'll be financially secure?

Fear 5 comes down to "If I stay at my current job, my financial script is written and predictable. If I do my own thing, who knows how this movie will end?" You've been trained for 30 years to believe in the power of the steady paycheck and you can't undo that thinking anytime soon.

Fear 6: You'd Rather Play It Safe Than Risk Failure

My father-in-law likes to tell the story of two mice looking for food in a locksmith store. The first mouse notices a trap with cheese in it. Rather than risk life and limb for a shot at the tasty cheese, he instead settles for licking the tasteless oil from the locksmith tools and machines. Oil is nowhere near a delicacy, but at least you'll make it out alive.

The second mouse gets one taste of the oil and says "This is not the life for me." He realizes there are some risks in snatching cheese from the trap. But a life without cheese simply isn't worth living.

Fear 6 says "Why should I go for something big when I could end up with nothing at all?" You'd rather guarantee some success than take a chance on bigger success with a risk of failing.

Fear 7: You Fear Breaking Your Current Routine

For years I listened to all my music on cassette tapes. My college roommates were quick to adapt to CDs, but I never wavered. They'd tell me the sound was better, you could skip right to your favorite song, and CD players could play multiple albums, not just one.

I was so used to rewinding and fast-forwarding cassette tapes I just couldn't break the routine even though something better came along. A new technology stood at my doorstep and I refused to answer the door.

Fear 7 comes down to "My routine might not be the best option, but I know how to do it and feel comfortable continuing on that path." You know there's a better way, but your current habit is so ingrained in your psyche you just can't let a new way of thinking penetrate that fortress.

Fear 8: You'll Lose the Approval of Friends and Family

You're at a dinner table with couples and a guy you never met asks the inevitable question ... "So what do you do for a living?" As a corporate climber you say, "I'm in marketing and sales" or "I'm a lawyer." Your new friend nods approvingly, passes the bread, and the night continues.

In your new life you won't be able to answer this ever-so-common question in three words or less. How do you say you invest in real estate, consult to corporations, write books, and sell products online in one easy-to-understand sentence? Instead you keep it simple and say you dabble in a bunch of businesses. Your dinner companion gives a quizzical look before buttering a roll under the assumption you're unemployed or embarrassed about your job.

Fear 8 says "People won't approve of me if they don't understand what I do, and nobody likes to go against society." You don't want to endure the uncomfortable questioning, so you stay in a profession people automatically respect.

> **Less Is More**
>
> When it comes to close friends and family, they worry about you. The more vulnerability you show, the more they'll assume you're unhappy and on the wrong path. Initially I shared my fears with all who would listen. I soon discovered that keeping some things to myself prevented undue pressure to give up my dream.

Fear 9: You're Afraid to Live in a Land of Ambiguity

It's Wednesday and here's what I did today. First I took my son swimming from 9 to 11 A.M. I then e-mailed back and forth with a potential tenant from 11 A.M. to noon. I met my wife for lunch at the office from noon to 2 P.M. From 2 to 4 P.M. I participated in a conference call with a consulting client. I met my parents for dinner before working on this chapter of the book from 8 to 10 P.M.

This day is nothing like my old life of sitting in a cubicle or office on Wednesday from 9 A.M. to 6 P.M. Sure that life was boring, but the predictability did provide comfort, and feeling comfortable is not to be underrated.

Fear 9 is all about "If I don't know what I'm doing each day, I'll feel uneasy and that tells me something is wrong." So you're willing to accept career unhappiness for the tradeoff of avoiding uncertainty day to day.

Fear 10: You're the One Getting in Your Own Way

Did you ever really want to do something big and your friends, family, and co-workers were all encouraging you to go for it? Maybe you're considering graduate school. Your friends want to help you with the application essays, your parents are willing to defray the tuition costs, and your boss is willing to write a letter of recommendation.

Somehow you talk yourself out of graduate school even though all your friends and supporters believe it's a great step. You actually convince yourself that all these people are somehow wrong and you're the only one who knows what's best for you.

Fear 10 says "My little voice wouldn't be talking me out of this move if it were right for me." So your objective friends, family, and co-workers get canceled out in favor of your inner monologue.

Solutions to Overcoming the Biggest Obstacles You'll Face

All 10 of these fears reared their ugly heads at some point in my journey from corporate employee to working less and earning more. The last thing I want to do is leave you hanging on how to battle back against these fears. That would be like ...

♦ Handing you a pile of sprinkles with no ice cream in sight.

♦ Telling you I just watched the best movie of the year without sharing the title.

♦ Stirring up all these fears in you without providing the tools and resources to overcome those fears and begin your journey toward working less and earning more.

So without further ado I'd like to share exactly how I overcame each of the 10 fears and how you can do the same. I hope you'll walk away from this section believing in yourself and realizing if I can overcome the fears you can do the same, too. By the way, these will not be tips like "believe in yourself" or "you can do it." This is meant to be a concrete guide, so I want to give you real-life solutions that will break down your fear walls and let working less and earning more enter your life.

1. Overcoming the Fear You Won't Be Able to Support Your Family

Here's a newsflash ... thanks to downsizing, constant company restructurings, and the lack of employee pensions, even the most dedicated corporate employee may not be able to support his or her family.

The sooner you can realize your steady job is no guarantee of steady lifetime income, the sooner you'll put less weight on your company controlling your ability to put food on the table. You need to untangle your current job from your ability to support your family. Where you work today represents just one of many options for making ends meet.

2. Overcoming the Fear You Won't Earn More Than Your Current Salary

For eight years I earned a paycheck. As long as I showed up Monday through Friday, my bank account automatically received a direct deposit every two weeks. This fear comes down to whether or not you believe someone will pay you directly for your expertise. When you're accustomed to a paycheck, it's hard to picture telling anyone you'll gladly write a PowerPoint presentation if they gladly deposit $5,000 in your account.

I overcame this fear by earning $75 to rewrite a resumé. I simply wanted to prove that someone would value my opinion enough to pay me directly. It took me approximately six hours of phone calls with the client and resumé rewrites to earn that $75. Making $12.50 per hour of work is not my idea of working less and earning more. Yet somehow depositing that $75 in my checking account meant more to me than a year's worth of paycheck direct deposits. Proving to myself I could get paid for my services demonstrated I had something worthwhile to offer the world. It wasn't long before my rates went up and the fear melted away that I could not only replace my salary but surpass it. Today, I can comfortably say "no" to this type of work, but it was a great way to build early confidence.

3. Overcoming the Fear You Don't Deserve to Work Less and Earn More

What you deserve in life is to be happy. How many people really believe they deserve to work longer hours for less compensation? I hope nobody who is reading this book.

Just because people around you will continue trudging to work every day doesn't mean you have to suffer the same fate. The more Tuesday tennis lessons, swim classes, and lazy lunches I've attended, the more people I've met who live a non–9-to-5 day. Keep surrounding yourself with these people and you'll stop noticing the corporate climbers in favor of those living the very life you desire. In fact, you can even check out one of my favorite sites, www.fourhourworkweek.com, to meet thousands of people who have escaped the 9-to-5 routine.

Ask Jeff _____

So if you truly deserve to work less and earn more, how much should you be working and how much should you be earning? My initial goal was to work half the time and maintain my old income. I then sought to cut the working time in half while doubling my income. Don't limit yourself. Set a goal to cut hours or increase revenue, then go for both simultaneously.

4. Overcoming the Fear You're Not Smart Enough

Do you remember that guy in Starbucks casually hunting and pecking on his laptop, wearing blue jeans, and sipping coffee seemingly without a care in the world? I admired that guy from afar, but something unexpected happened when I gathered the courage to talk to him. I found out I went to a better college than he did. I learned I had more corporate experience than he did. I discovered he was working on a proposal to score more business because new leads had been light this year.

Summing it all up, I was better educated, more experienced, and less in need of a sale compared to this guy. But somehow I had built him up in my mind because he looked so casual and carefree as he lounged in Starbucks.

I've since learned to show some self-respect for my education, experience, and personal achievements. This is not about arrogance. It's about realizing that judging a book by its cover means you haven't checked out the content of the book. That guy in Starbucks initially intimidated me, but I eventually realized that if he could look so casual and self-satisfied, I could, too.

5. Overcoming the Fear That You Were Raised to Believe in a Steady Paycheck

The smartest thing my wife and I did when I contemplated a career change was to save up six months of living expenses. We stashed this cash away in a money-market account. We then agreed we would not blame each other if my journey fell flat and we burned through that six-month cushion.

Immediately the pressure was lifted off earning income right away. I knew I had six full months to generate revenue. I also knew there'd be no blame or resentment if my journey failed. Guess what happened? With the pressure to earn right away alleviated, I made better long-term decisions and never touched that money.

Less Is More

The less you have to worry about money, the more likely you are to really go for working less and earning more. That's why the six-month cushion is so important. If you had only one week of reserves set aside, you'd probably take the first gig that came your way. But would that gig necessarily get you any closer to the life you desire? Check out www.money.aol.com/calculators for some automatic savings calculators that are easy to use.

6. Overcoming the Fear That You'd Rather Play It Safe Than Risk Failure

If you're a safety-first guy like me, you need to let a little risk seep into your life. That's not to say you should skydive in the morning, bungee jump in the afternoon, and wrestle alligators by nightfall. But you do need to take a few risks to see the bigger payoff that sometimes awaits. For example, on our honeymoon my wife somehow convinced me to rappel 300 feet down into a cave. This was fully supervised and closer to a Disney World ride than man against nature. But it still scared me. It's been years now since our honeymoon, but that experience stands out first in my mind. It's one of my most vivid memories.

The risks often become the defining moments in your life. This doesn't mean bet your life savings on one turn of the roulette wheel. But it does mean that a few calculated risks have a way of leapfrogging your life experiences and opening new doors.

7. Overcoming the Fear of Breaking Your Current Routine

Right now I want you to think about one antiquated habit you've been following for years. For me it was a love for cassette tapes. What's your habit that refuses to rest in peace? Do you use a hard-copy planner instead of a Palm Treo? Do you drive to work every day even though the train would be twice as fast? Do you still wear your old clothes despite the fact your favorite shirts could disintegrate the next time you run the wash?

Pick that one habit and decide today to give it up cold turkey. Buy your first CD. Go shopping for a Treo. Take the train to work tomorrow morning. Kiss that disintegrating shirt good-bye and treat yourself to a trendy new replacement. I guarantee you'll wonder why you didn't act sooner. You'll laugh at yourself for letting old habits die hard when better solutions stared you in the face for months or years.

8. Overcoming the Fear You'll Lose the Approval of Friends and Family

I admit I used to feel uncomfortable at dinner parties. I knew the "what do you do for a living" question would rear its ugly head. I could feel that bead of sweat form on my temple as folks went around the room saying "doctor," "lawyer," or "businessman."

Then one day I simply gave myself permission to not care how people judged my answer. Sure it was 15 seconds of feeling uncomfortable. But soon enough my dinner companions would shift their attention to hearing the daily specials. I was the one building this question up to be some monumental weigh-in on my career decision.

The sooner you realize you are the one living your career decision, not friends and family, the sooner you release yourself from caring so much about other people's opinions.

Fear Busters _____

After one too many uncomfortable dinner parties, I developed a 30-second elevator speech to answer the dreaded "what do you do for a living" question. I simply said "I'm a business consultant as well as a writer, speaker, and coach in the areas of relationships, career advancement, and personal development." Having a script alleviated the fears of this question and helped me respond with confidence. Often people were intrigued by an answer that didn't sound like doctor, lawyer, or accountant.

9. Overcoming the Fear That You Can't Live in a Land of Ambiguity

Do you remember how I described my Wednesday? Activities included swimming with my son, talking to potential tenants, lunch with my wife, a consulting conference call, dinner with the folks, and writing a chapter of this book. Could this day be any more disjointed and ambiguous? Not really, but it also didn't feel like work to me.

Between the swimming, lunch with my wife, and dinner with Mom and Dad, I hardly minded the tenant communication, consulting call, and writing slot. The less that work feels like work, the more you're on the right track toward working less and earning more. In fact, if you can make work feel enjoyable as it does for me when I'm writing, even working time begins to feel like you're not working. That's a welcome addition to the working-less, earning-more lifestyle.

10. Overcoming the Fear That You're the One Getting in Your Own Way

For one day and one day only tell yourself you don't get a vote. So when the little voice speaks up, say "thank you for the advice, but today you're on a day off so grab a towel, sit by the pool, and let me go about my business."

You see, the little voice is helpful and hurtful. The little voice can tell you to run when you see a bear. But it also can tell you you're not good enough, smart enough, or driven enough to be successful. So unless you're alone in the woods today with a high risk of bear sightings, please hit the mute button on your little voice for one day. You'll be amazed how many life experiences it was stopping you from enjoying.

How to Build Your Network to Make the Transition

Do any of these phrases sound familiar to you?

♦ It's every man for himself.

♦ It's a dog-eat-dog world out there.

♦ You're the only real friend you've got.

♦ If you want something done right, do it yourself.

♦ *The Complete Idiot's Guide to Working Less, Earning More* is the best book of all time.

Okay, so maybe just the first four phrases have been ingrained in your psyche since birth. Perhaps after reading this book you'll include the fifth bullet, too. Wishful thinking I suppose, but a guy can dream!

What do these phrases have in common? They all assume you're on your own in the cold, dark world. I must admit, when I left corporate America I bought into this myth. After all, I was now a sole proprietor. Sole means "one" so I guess I'm alone out there. I mistakenly believed my success depended solely on my personal effort. Boy was I wrong. Here's a quick snapshot of the people who helped me achieve my greatest successes:

♦ **Buying a two-family house:** Rather than scouring the seller listings or working with the first agent I could find, I contacted a local real estate office that connected me with its two-family specialist. He patiently explained the strategies behind buying a two-family house with positive cash flow and took me to see the right properties. He has become an important part of my network, and I would not buy another property without him.

◆ **Landing this book deal:** I've become friendly with a well-connected innovation consultant. We have become part of each other's network and make sure to catch up periodically. I casually mentioned to him I was looking to write more extensively in the field of career and life transitions. He happened to get a call from a literary agent looking for a new writer on this topic and instantly thought of me.

Time and a Half _____

Almost everyone has a book idea in their head. If you're looking to turn that idea into a real page turner, I recommend attending the Book Expo of America (www.bookexpoamerica.com). Held once per year, the Expo gathers together every publisher in the industry. I went to that conference as an aspiring writer and left with a strong publishing lead that turned into my first book deal.

◆ **Writing freelance online articles:** My wife and I have a friend who works for a major online content and information provider. She let us know the site was looking for a new writer to cover the dating and relationship category, and I was able to compete for the position that I would not have known about otherwise.

◆ **Consulting to Fortune 500 companies:** I met a fellow member at a National Speaker's Association meeting who told me about a site called Guru.com. On this site you can post your credentials and search for consulting or freelance gigs that match your skills. Through Guru.com I contacted an HR-consulting company and have since completed multiple assignments for Fortune 500 companies.

Less Is More _____

Perhaps you're a highly qualified, talented mom looking to reenter the workforce after raising kids. You know you want to work less than full-time to spend more time with your family. You can check out momcorps.com for a full listing of flexible, part-time, and work-from-home opportunities designed to match projects to your capabilities.

◆ **Presenting in front of 1,000 people:** My friend in California works in radio sales. Every year his company puts together a huge conference on personal health and well-being. My friend arranged a dinner for me with the conference organizer. Over Coronas and mozzarella sticks we mapped out a unique presentation topic, and I scored a keynote address at the conference.

These are examples of some of my biggest successes to date. All five would absolutely have been impossible without help from someone else. From this day forward I would like to rewrite those old and worn-out phrases as follows:

"It's every man for himself" will now be "It's every man for every man."

"It's a dog-eat-dog world out there" will now be "It's a dog-meet-dog world out there."

"You're the only real friend you've got" will now be "You've got more real friends than you can invite to a dinner party."

"If you want something done right, do it yourself" will now be "If you want something done right, do it together."

I shared my success stories for only one reason. I want to debunk the myth that doing your own thing literally means doing your own thing. I made this mistake the first three months after leaving corporate America. I soon learned that buying properties, scoring book deals, writing freelance, consulting to large companies, and presenting to thousands would be difficult without leaving my sofa.

Less Is More _____

It is truly liberating when you first break away from the office and score a work-from-home assignment. By all means soak up the ability to take conference calls in your pajamas. After the novelty wears off, you'll feel the urge to be around people again. I now strive for fewer days at home and more time in Starbucks or with clients just for the people interaction, and often for the doors that continue to open as a result.

As you consider the transition to working less and earning more, I hope I've officially saved you three months on your journey. The most important first success step is to build a network of people that can help you. For the introverts out there, I know exactly what you're thinking. Making new friends is tiring and not your specialty.

Guess what? I'm an introvert, too. I'll prove it to you. Pretend I walked into a room and saw four people:

♦ An A-list celebrity who just starred in a major movie

♦ My favorite baseball player on my favorite team

♦ A generous-looking person handing out $100 bills

♦ My best friend who lives down the block

 Time and a Half

Go to www.myersbriggs.org and take the personality profile test. You'll find out where you sit on the introvert/extrovert spectrum as well as how to successfully connect with people whether you're the life of the party or a wallflower.

I can tell you without hesitation you'll find me in the corner talking to my best friend. I just turned down a chance to meet a celebrity, get an autograph from my baseball idol, and possibly make free money. If I can build a solid, wide network, so can you. I'm going to make it easy for you with a five-step plan to build a network of over 1,000 people in less than a week.

Step 1: Get Clear on the Help You Need

Pull up to a gas station and say, "Can you help me with directions?" The attendant will likely say, "Sure, where are you headed?" If you can't answer this question, the gas station attendant becomes a useless ally. Now picture pulling up to a gas station and saying, "Can you help me find Route 95 North?" Now you have a clear goal in mind and the attendant is likely to help if he or she possesses the right information. If not, you might get pointed to someone else who can help you, which is good, too.

Before you reach out to your first contact for help, you've got to get clear on the specific help you need. Are you trying to get into real estate? If so, in what capacity? Do you want to flip properties for profit, buy foreclosures, or invest in rental properties to earn cash flow? The more specific you get, the better help you'll receive.

Step 2: Make a List of Everyone You Know

Before making this list I mistakenly assumed I knew maybe 20 or 30 people. My list ended up with over 1,000 people. How did I build this list? Five resources made all the difference:

- ◆ My wedding invite list contained over 200 names.

- ◆ My holiday-card list contained over 150 additional names.

- ◆ My online e-mail address book contained over 400 names.

- ◆ My high school and college yearbooks reminded me of over 100 old friends from back in the day.

- ◆ My Rolodex at work contained over 150 business cards.

It took me less than two hours to compile these 1,000 names into a spreadsheet of possible contacts. I then developed a rudimentary 1, 2, 3 scoring system to rank the likelihood of each person helping me reach my goals. For example, my 94-year old grandma earned a "3," while my college roommate running a successful small business earned a "1." Don't get me wrong; I love my grandma, but her best connections these days involve hot games of gin rummy.

My Excel spreadsheet automatically sorted my contact list, putting all the "1's" at the top of the list. I now had a hit list of my best contacts.

Step 3: Ask Everyone You Know Who They Know

Have you ever played Six Degrees of Separation? Rumor has it you can link any Hollywood celebrity to Kevin Bacon in six steps or fewer. Networking works the same way. It's not just who you know but who the people you know network with, too. That's how a list of 1,000 contacts can grow to 3,000 or 5,000 in no time.

Here's a quick example. In Step 2, I mentioned my old college roommate who started a successful small business. He was a great contact in sharing the ups and downs of running your own show. But he also happened to have a close friend from graduate school who was a motivational speaker. My roommate connected me to this friend, and the speaker spent two hours explaining to me how you break into the motivational speaking business.

Ask Jeff _____

Is it really okay to contact nearly everyone you know and ask for assistance? People mistake asking for help with being a mooch. You're not asking to borrow money; you're looking for a push in the right direction. You'll quickly find out that most people want to be helpful and get a sense of satisfaction from doing a good deed. Be sure to show your appreciation by offering to help them in return should they need it someday.

Step 4: Join One Relevant Industry Association

You've got to join at least one industry association that closely relates to your working-less, earning-more goals. One of the first places I joined was the National Speaker's Association because I wanted to give seminars. By attending monthly meetings, I learned ...

- ◆ How to sign up with speaker's bureaus that can help me get booked at conferences.

- ◆ How to build a website that effectively communicates my speaking expertise.

- ◆ How to create information products, like e-books and CDs, that I can sell online to supplement my speaking income.

- ◆ How to sum up my keynote address topic in 30 seconds or less for potential clients.

- ◆ How to add humor and personal experiences to my seminars to make them more interesting for the audience.

Step 5: Join One Online Networking or Prospecting Site

For this step you can go with a purely networking site like www. LinkedIn.com or a site that helps you prospect for gigs like www.Guru. com. I'm personally a bigger fan of the prospecting sites because there's a more direct connection to earning money.

I listed my human-resources experience on www.Guru.com and received e-mails every day with potential consulting projects that met my skills and expertise. After six leads failed to pan out, the seventh led to that fruitful consulting relationship with the human-resources consulting firm I mentioned earlier.

Generating Early Momentum to Build Self-Confidence

The official motto of working less and earning more is "ready, fire, aim." All I've done is swap the last two words in a popular phrase and change its meaning entirely. While I don't recommend this approach when hunting or playing archery, it's a great motto for this book.

I can usually tell in 10 minutes or less if someone will take any action toward working less and earning more. If they get caught up in all the "what if" scenarios and overplanning, they'll never get off the ground. I, too, made this mistake early on before realizing that small actions create momentum and get the ball rolling. In the early months, I focused on ...

- ◆ Designing the perfect business card complete with a creative logo and unique slogan.

- ◆ Crafting a detailed 12-month action plan with sophisticated check boxes and weekly status updates.

- ◆ Writing 50 pages of a self-help book that I believed would be a bestseller.

I'm not one to argue that business cards, action plans, and kick-starting a book are worthy endeavors. However, all three have something in common ... zero income! Let's be honest, anyone can work less. All you have to do is stop showing up for work. It's the earning-more part that trips up most folks. That's where "ready, fire, aim" comes in handy. Instead of logging countless hours in planning mode, you dive right into earning money.

Let's spin these three bullets to make them more revenue-focused:

- You focus your energy on landing that first client and then create the business card to give to him or her.

> **Time and a Half**
>
> Once you're ready to design business cards, don't waste time shopping for the right business-card designer. I highly recommend iPrint.com. For about $30 you can upload a logo, choose from hundreds of card designs, lay out your contact information, and receive 250 high-quality business cards in about one week. These cards look better than anything I ever carried during my days in corporate America.

- You take action for one or two weeks, see what's working for you, and then build a detailed action plan from there.

- You write a book proposal and shop it around to agents and publishers who can guide you on the actual book content.

There is an undeniable connection between small victories and self-confidence. Spend all your time in planning, and you'll worry yourself right into inertia. Jump in right away and correct your course when necessary, and you'll be on your way to working less and earning more.

Here are the smartest small steps I took for each of my revenue channels to generate momentum and build on the early wins:

- **Public speaking:** I contacted my local continuing education department and inquired about teaching a class next semester. Do you remember watching Tom Cruise grill Jack Nicholson on the stand in *A Few Good Men*? My interview experience with the community center was the exact opposite. They were excited to have a new teacher and even helped me brainstorm topics that would draw students.

Fear Busters _____

So you want to get into public speaking but you'd rather sit through a root canal? I've got two great ways to face those fears head on. First, you can join Toastmasters (www.toastmasters.org). This low-pressure organization teaches public speaking from the ground up. Second, you could take a stand-up comedy class. You'll learn how to write original material, the importance of timing, and how to get laughs from the audience.

♦ **Writing a book:** As I mentioned before, I called a friend who recently published a book and asked him how to score a book deal. He urged me to attend the Book Expo of America, where I met an interested publisher for my book.

♦ **Consulting:** Writing a resumé and earning $75 proved someone cared about my advice and would pay for my services. Sure it wasn't $2,000 per day, but when you've never been paid directly for your work, anything is a good start.

♦ **Online products:** I bought an e-book called *The Seven Day Guide to Creating and Marketing Your Own E-Book*. This e-book wiped away the mystery of selling e-books online, and sure enough I had created my own in about one week.

♦ **Real estate investing:** I contacted my local real estate office, got connected with that two-family house expert, and quickly got up to speed on how to buy a two-family property to generate positive cash flow.

Let's break down these five examples. I didn't know my public-speaking topic, didn't have a book idea, had never written a resumé for someone, had barely heard of e-books, and never looked at a two-family house in my life. The point is you don't need to be an expert before you take those baby steps. If I had waited to master my speaking topic, flesh out my book, gain advanced credentials in resumé writing, get a Master's in online marketing, or earn my real estate license, I'd still be in planning mode.

However you decide to work less and earn more, be sure to hit the ground running. Believe me, those early wins will set the stage for bigger victories.

The Least You Need to Know

◆ Grizzly bears cause fear, but changing jobs only causes anxiety—
you need to know the difference.

◆ Most fears are unfounded and can be conquered through taking
action toward a well-defined goal.

◆ Contrary to popular belief, most people are helpful and are willing to give their time and energy if you clearly articulate where
you want to go.

◆ It's amazing how one small victory sends your confidence through
the roof and pushes you to go after bigger and grander goals.

Five Paths to Working Less and Earning More

Wanting to work less and earn more is a noble aspiration. But how do you actually make it happen? Daydreaming at your cubicle about a better life is not likely to achieve the results you desire. That's why Part 2 of this book breaks down five realistic paths to working less and earning more.

We start with the path of least resistance … staying in your current job. From there, we look at becoming a consultant, working freelance, running a business, and earning passive income. Any of these five paths can turn the most overworked, underpaid person into a working-less, earning-more machine. In fact, you can even incorporate more than one of these paths into a balanced and diversified approach to working and earning.

Chapter 4

Staying in Your Job Without Staying in a Rut

In This Chapter

♦ Deciding whether your job can ever meet the criteria of working less and earning more

♦ Becoming so valuable at work your boss practically begs you to begin a flexible working arrangement instead of losing you to a competitor

♦ Convincing your boss the work won't suffer if you're not sitting in your cubicle 50 hours per week

♦ Staying in your job while still working less

I just spent the last few chapters convincing you to walk away from your cushy job and go for a working-less, earning-more lifestyle. In Chapters 5 through 8, we cover four main strategies for making this dream a reality.

Before you give your two-weeks' notice and launch a business, become a real estate mogul, open your consulting practice, or market products online, I get that some folks flat-out do not want to leave their job. You're looking to have your cake and eat it, too. You want to keep the security of a steady paycheck while still creating a more favorable work scenario. If that sounds like you, Chapter 4 is dedicated to you.

One caveat you should know going into this chapter: I've seen tons of folks stay in their job, work less, and maintain their income. However, working less and earning more is a tall order while remaining with your company. Still, if you told me I could keep my same salary and cut my hours 20 to 30 percent, I'd take that deal in a heartbeat.

So let's get started on how to stay in your job or with your same company while working fewer hours. In this chapter, you learn how to decipher whether or not your company favors flexible working arrangements. You also find out how to approach your boss to make it a reality for you. Then I go into three of the most popular flexible arrangements, including virtual offices, compressed workweeks, and mini-vacations.

Does Your Job Have Working-Less, Earning-More Potential?

Not every caterpillar becomes a butterfly, and not every company can offer you a flexible arrangement. In this chapter, we refer to flexible arrangements as any working setup that doesn't require you to sit at your cubicle or office desk five days per week, 50 weeks per year.

You've got to know whether it's even possible before you go down the road. Here's a quick questionnaire to help you learn the truth about your own company. Answer yes or no to the following questions.

Will Your Company Support a Flexible Arrangement?

1. Does your company maintain an intranet where you could look up policies on requesting a flexible working arrangement?

  ____ Yes   ____ No

2. Has your human resources department ever issued a memo or guidebook announcing flexible working arrangements?

    ___ Yes   ___ No

3. Are you aware of any departments in your company ever experimenting with virtual offices, compressed workweeks, or paid sabbaticals?

    ___ Yes   ___ No

4. Have any of your colleagues ever requested and been granted a flexible working arrangement?

    ___ Yes   ___ No

5. Do any departments in your company work virtually (i.e., the sales force)?

    ___ Yes   ___ No

6. Is your company typically ahead of the curve when it comes to adopting new employee policies?

    ___ Yes   ___ No

7. Is your boss open-minded and willing to listen to alternative points of view and new ideas?

    ___ Yes   ___ No

8. Is your boss's supervisor open-minded and willing to listen to alternative points of view and new ideas?

    ___ Yes   ___ No

9. Have you ever been allowed to work from home for a few days to focus on completing a big project or deliverable?

    ___ Yes   ___ No

10. Does your gut tell you your company would be open to your request for a flexible working arrangement?

    ___ Yes   ___ No

> **Time and a Half** _____
>
> Let's say you have no idea whether flexible arrangements exist at your company. The quickest way to find out is to use the search feature on your company intranet (if you have one). Search for flexible arrangements, virtual office policies, sabbaticals, or any other term that might lead you to company policies on the subject. If you're looking to learn the basics, check out www.FlexPaths.com for an introduction to flexible arrangements.

You should now have some combination of "yes" and "no" responses checked off in this worksheet. Let's tally the numbers:

- Between seven and ten "yes" responses: Congratulations! Your environment is ripe for a flexible arrangement. You just might be a simple request away from scoring a great new work scenario.

- Between four and six "yes" responses: I have good news and bad news! The good news is your company has shown signs of a willingness to consider flexible arrangements. The bad news is your score is too low to consider it a sure thing.

- Between zero and three "yes" responses: Uh Oh! You're barking up the wrong tree. It sounds like flexibility is a foreign concept or at least not very common to your company.

The reality is any job has the potential for a flexible arrangement. It's just that if your company has no history of it, nobody has ever requested one, and there's no policy, then this is an uphill climb. The hill might be so steep you're actually better off switching departments or finding a new job before you entertain flexible arrangement thoughts.

I was teaching my seminar called "Take Charge of Your Career," and a hand went up in the audience. A young lady said, "I really want to work virtually, but my boss flat-out refuses to consider my request. What should I do?" I told her the same thing I'm going to tell you now. There's a three-step answer to this question:

Step 1: Can you convince your boss to reconsider his or her position on virtual offices?

Step 2: If not, can you move to a different department that might be more open to a flexible arrangement?

Step 3: If not, would you be willing to find a new job in a company that already offers flexible arrangements?

The young lady looked at me and said, "No, no, and no." The crowd laughed, but I shot back with a bonus step:

Step 4: Are you willing to make peace with staying in your current position and never working virtually?

Fear Busters _____

There's a difference between fearing your boss won't consider a flexible arrangement and knowing your boss won't agree to one. Before you dismiss asking your boss, ask yourself if you're just building up anxiety for no reason. Often these conversations go better than you anticipate. Remember, bosses are people, too, with families, hobbies, and a life outside the office. Check out www.WorkOptions.com if you want to see actual script templates you can use to talk to your boss.

Not surprisingly, the answer was a resounding "no" again. The crowd chuckled, half expecting me to keep adding steps until the answer changed to "yes." But my list ends with Step 4. Answering "no" to all four steps is like living on a one-way, dead-end street. You'll never get out of the situation. So the reality is you have to answer "yes" to one of these steps.

Because your goal in this chapter is to transition to a flexible arrangement, my goal is to help you figure out the easiest way to do it. Can you convince your boss, do you need to change departments, or do you have to find a new job first? Go for whichever seems both the easiest to attempt and the most likely to lead where you want to go.

Becoming Indispensable Before Seeking a New Work Scenario

Here's a tale of two employees ....

Joanna is a hard worker. She's diligent, dedicated, and detail-oriented. She never misses deliverables or deadlines. She's proactive on the job, volunteering for new assignments, and always pitching in to lend a hand. She rarely calls in sick. In fact, she's typically at her desk by 8:30 A.M. to get a jump on her day. When Joanna's boss needs something done right, she knows she can count on Joanna.

John is a bit of a slacker. He's absent-minded, undedicated, and lacks attention to detail. He frequently misses deliverables and deadlines. He's reactive on the job, grudgingly accepting new assignments, and rarely pitching in to lend a hand. He frequently calls in sick. In fact, he typically rolls into work around 9:30 or 9:45 A.M. to ease into his day. When John's boss needs something done right, she knows she can't count on John.

Here are two questions for you ....

> Question 1: Which employee is more likely to get approval for a flexible working arrangement?

> Question 2: Which employee sounds more like you?

I hope you answered "Joanna" to both questions. If you answered "John" to both questions, then I don't foresee a flexible arrangement in your future. I do see a negative performance review, a development plan, and potentially a one-way ticket to the unemployment office unless you step up your game.

Ask Jeff

How do you really know if you're viewed as Joanna or John in the office? Your most recent performance review is a great way to find out. The next best option is 360-degree feedback if your company has a process for employees to gather feedback from peers, leaders, and subordinates. If neither option exists, take a trusted colleague to lunch and ask for an honest assessment.

I've got to be honest. I have never met anyone who thinks they're a "John," but we all know "John" exists in every office. So maybe you're not exactly John, but could you qualify as a distant cousin? You see, bosses, departments, and companies that offer flexible arrangements always have one concern. They want to make sure your work and that of the team won't suffer. So they naturally ask questions about both your performance and that of the role you inhabit. The better they feel about these questions, the more likely they are to consider a flexible arrangement.

Questions Your Boss Will Ask About Your Performance

Do you meet deadlines?	Yes/No
Do you work well with minimal supervision?	Yes/No
Are you a motivated self-starter?	Yes/No
Do you effectively communicate via phone?	Yes/No
Can you adapt to a changing work environment?	Yes/No
Are you good at building relationships and networks?	Yes/No
Do you earn high marks on performance reviews?	Yes/No
Have you earned the respect of your colleagues?	Yes/No
Are you willing to work extra to get the job done?	Yes/No
Do you focus on the job and avoid distractions?	Yes/No

As you can imagine, the more "yes" responses, the more you sound like "Joanna" and the less you sound like "John." In essence, your boss and company want to know that you could still get the job done without the structure of a desk, cubicle, in-person meetings, and a boss looking over your shoulder. By the way, these "yes" responses will be your best evidence you can successfully pull off a flexible arrangement when it comes time to officially ask your boss for permission.

Less Is More

Many bosses have a simple equation for determining your performance. The fewer headaches you create for them, the more they value you. In other words, the fewer problems you bring to their attention and the more solutions you provide, the higher your value. Think about what you value in people who work for you; it's a great start in how to effectively interact with your boss.

If you want to set yourself up for earning a flexible working arrangement, I urge you to take a close look at the questions your boss will ask about your performance. If you're falling short in multiple areas, now is the time to make improvements. Otherwise you're headed for a less-than-enthusiastic response from management.

Keep in mind, it's not just you who matters here but also the role you play at work. Your boss and company will ask questions about your job to see if a flexible arrangement makes sense.

Questions Your Boss Will Ask About Your Role

Can your role be performed with limited face-to-face interactions with co-workers, leaders, and clients?	Yes/No
Can your role be performed in varying locations?	Yes/No
Can your role be done at various times of the day?	Yes/No
Does your role require minimal supervision?	Yes/No
Are some or all of your team members virtual?	Yes/No
Will the team manage sufficiently if you're not onsite to guide them day to day?	Yes/No
Can projects be completed with phone-based check-ins between you and team members?	Yes/No
Would work carry on successfully if you were not present for a few days or weeks?	Yes/No
Does the technology exist to keep you connected to get the job done?	Yes/No
Will other team members likely view your flexible arrangement in a positive way?	Yes/No

If you haven't guessed by now, "yes" responses are key. Your boss and company want to know that you and your team will fully function despite the change in your work arrangement. They want to feel like your new arrangement won't make the team skip even a beat.

Putting both tables together, four possibilities exist:

◆ Possibility 1: Your performance and the role are ripe for a flexible arrangement. If this sounds like you, stand up right now and scream, "I'm outta here!" Then apologize to your cubicle neighbor for screaming with no warning.

♦ Possibility 2: Your performance warrants flexibility, but the role is not right for it. I'd like to congratulate you for demonstrating the skills required for flexibility. Now it's time to think about changing departments or positions to land a role that warrants a flexible arrangement.

♦ Possibility 3: Your role warrants flexibility, but your performance does not. Look in the mirror because staring back at you is the person responsible for preventing a flexible arrangement. I know you can raise your game, so get to it and flexibility is your reward.

♦ Possibility 4: Both your performance and the role are not right for a flexible arrangement. Uh oh! That steep hill is back again. Raising your game and changing jobs is a tall order.

The bottom line is that indispensable employees in roles that warrant flexibility are most likely to earn the right. Before you even approach your boss you've got to take that honest look at both your recent performance and the nature of your role. Once you're considered a high-potential employee in a role built for flexibility, you've set yourself up to hear "absolutely" when you ask for a new arrangement.

Approaching Your Boss to Pitch a New Working Arrangement

If you haven't guessed by now, I don't recommend asking for a flexible arrangement the day after you read this chapter of the book. You've got to set the groundwork, become indispensable, and show your boss and company the role won't suffer.

In this section, I lay out a nine-step progressive plan to successfully approach your boss within 90 days. Why 9 steps instead of 10? Well, the best I could come up with for step 10 was to give it your all. Let's leave the inspirational mumbo-jumbo to the motivational speeches and focus instead on the nuts and bolts of getting to "yes" with your boss. Why 90 days? Well, three months seems like a long time, but 90 days will fly by. Besides, 90 days is enough time to completely revamp your image in the office.

One caveat to this plan: I'm going to assume you're already in a role that has the potential for a flexible arrangement. If not, before you undertake this action plan you really need to either change roles in your company or look for a new job. Otherwise you're about to implement a plan with no chance of success. This plan also works best when shooting for the virtual arrangement because that's my top choice in the land of flexible arrangements (I'll explain why later in this chapter). But you can easily adapt the steps if you're more interested in a compressed workweek or mini-vacation (i.e., paid sabbatical).

Step 1: Avoid Complaining and Negativity

Nobody likes a complainer. Nobody wants to be around negative people. It's a downer and it kills your mood. Before you even think about a flexible arrangement, put a smile on your face. Why do you think politicians smile so much? It's not to show off their dental work. Politicians know that more smiling equals more votes.

The same holds true in the workplace. A simple smile can change people's perception of you. Package that up with eliminating negativity and complaining and you'll win the award for Mr. or Ms. Congeniality. When people think more favorably of you, they're more open to saying "yes" to your requests. This holds true particularly for bosses, so show those pearly whites.

Step 2: Get Yourself Organized

A simple smile is a great start, but it won't get your boss to sign on the dotted line. The next step is to organize your key deliverables for the next 90 days. What are the five most important projects you need to complete? How could you over-deliver on these projects and surpass expectations?

The goal here is for nothing to fall through the cracks and your work to "wow the crowd." If you can't meet or exceed expectations in the office, why would your boss ever consider handing you more freedom? If anything, your boss will turn on the micromanaging, so get those big deliverables under control.

Time and a Half _____

If your e-mail inbox has 534 unread messages, your voicemail is full, and your desk is the Mount Rushmore of paperwork, getting organized can overwhelm you. You don't have to read and listen to everything to get the upper hand on your assignments. Simply scan the subjects of e-mails, listen to the first sentence of voicemails, and read the headlines on paperwork. In less than an hour you can generate a simple list of your top deliverables.

Step 3: Go Above and Beyond Your Role

Now we're off and running. You're smiling ear to ear while over-delivering on your five biggest projects. That's a great start, but let's take it up a notch and make your boss's job easier, too. Try a simple line like, "Hey boss, your plate seems overloaded right now. Care to hand me an extra project or two so you can make your kid's little league game this week?" If your boss doesn't fall out of her chair in disbelief, it's only because she's too busy handing you files from her desk.

Pull off this strategy and you've got double-barrel action going. You're dominating on your own work while simultaneously making your supervisor's life easier. I can see it now. Your boss slides into the bleachers next to a neighbor and says, "You're not going to believe this, but Joanna offered to finish up one of my projects so I could duck out early and see little Lisa smack a double." The neighbor can't help but say, "Wow, Joanna is a real go-getter. Don't lose her from your team."

Step 4: Do One Thing Flexibly

Steps 1, 2, and 3 were all about portraying a positive image, delivering big-time on your assignments, and helping your boss. Now it's time to stick our toe in the flexibility pool. You don't need a formal meeting to make it happen. Instead, casually say to your boss something like, "You know that PowerPoint presentation I'm cranking out for Friday? Do you think I could work from home the next two days to really focus and avoid office distractions?"

Remember, thanks to steps 1, 2, and 3, your boss knows you're a go-getter. Don't be surprised when the response goes something like, "You know what, that's not a bad idea. This presentation is really important so if you can focus better at home, go for it." When you get the go-ahead, be sure to write one of the best presentations of all time. Otherwise you just sabotaged yourself. Also, check in once or twice per day from home so your boss knows you are really working and doesn't think you're pulling a Ferris Bueller. (You know, pretending to be home when you're really at the Cubs game, singing "Twist and Shout" in a parade, and dining at five-star restaurants.)

Step 5: Point Out the Upside

Your flexible arrangement game plan is front and center for you, but your boss is not clued in. He may be so busy he doesn't even remember agreeing to a few workdays from home. It's your job to resurface the discussion and note the upside.

Wait until your boss gives you kudos for a presentation well done. Then casually remark, "It's amazing how much better I worked without the constant interruption of phone calls, meetings, and folks popping by my cubicle. I really dove into the presentation and put my full energy behind it." It's a jackpot if your boss says you should work from home more often. But the more likely response is, "I'm glad it worked out for you." That's okay, you really just want to make sure your boss isn't putting the kibosh on your plan before it takes off.

Less Is More

When you lay out the upside of working flexibly, don't pile on 23 reasons. It will look like you're grasping for anything that will stick. Go for two or three solid reasons, especially things that would be important to your boss. Have persuasive examples that demonstrate the upside of your flexible arrangement. You'll come across as confident, prepared, and logical instead of unsure, unprepared, and scatter-brained.

Step 6: Request a Trial Period

Your goal in step six is to turn a one-time thing into a trial period. For your next PowerPoint deliverable, ask for the same two days from home. When your boss says okay, take the bait and say, "You know, I work on so many of these presentations, two days from home each week would really make a big difference."

Your boss may go for it or hesitate. If you sense wavering, immediately offer a two-week trial period. Suggest that you work from home Tuesday and Wednesday this week and next. After the trial period you'll check in together to see if the plan is working. By now, you've laid enough groundwork that hopefully your boss will see no harm in a two-week trial run.

Step 7: Gather Feedback from Your Boss

Be true to your word in step 7 and set up time to reflect on the two-week trial period. Remind your boss how happy she was with your work. Demonstrate how you stayed connected via phone and e-mail. Casually mention that one of your direct reports feels the team didn't even skip a beat. Don't force your opinion on your boss, just cover your bases.

Your boss will weigh in. Listen carefully to what your boss believes could have gone better. Then suggest another two-week trial and make clear you'll focus on her feedback.

Step 8: Take the Feedback Seriously

So what did your boss say could have been better? Did he want to talk to you last Wednesday at 2 P.M. but couldn't track you down? Did your Internet connection at home falter and you couldn't e-mail a presentation to your boss for feedback?

Whatever went wrong … fix it fast! Give your boss your cell phone number to call you any time for immediate access to you on work-from-home days. Bring your broadband provider out to

Fear Busters

People are so afraid of feedback. We all want that approval stamp from those in power positions. But you really need to get inside your boss's head to know where he sees snags in your flexible plan. So instead see the feedback as a blessing because it gives you clear-cut marching orders to make the necessary tweaks to eventually gain permanent flexibility approval.

your home to check the connection and eliminate technical difficulties. Step 8 is about eliminating the obvious objections from your boss to make "no" an unlikely answer when you go for the permanent flexible arrangement.

Step 9: Make the Arrangement Permanent

Now it's time to put it all together. You're smiling every day, you're over-delivering on projects, you've taken on some of your boss's work, you've successfully worked virtually, you've asked for feedback, you've ironed out the kinks, and you've eliminated potential objections to a permanent arrangement.

Ninety days have passed, and it's time to ask for the trial period to become your new way of life. If your company has an official flexible arrangement policy, be sure to read it thoroughly to understand the process for approval. Now get in there and close the deal with your boss. The good news is that steps 1 through 8 set the foundation to give yourself the best possible chance of making it so.

Jackpot Scenario 1: The Virtual Office

The next three sections of this chapter cover three top options for a flexible arrangement:

- ♦ The virtual office
- ♦ The compressed workweek
- ♦ The extended vacation or paid sabbatical

For each flexible arrangement, I'll define it, give the advantages, and of course explain the downside, too (hey, a guy has to be honest). Remember, working less and earning more is tough to pull off while staying at the same company. After all, can you really tell your boss you want to double your income and cut your hours in half? So we're focused instead on flexible arrangements that can maintain your income while easing the hours you spend at your desk. Let's start with the virtual office and get this flexible party started!

The Definition

The virtual office, often called telecommuting, is any arrangement where your primary office is not the desk you currently inhabit. Don't try to pull a fast one on me here and claim that moving to the desk next to you would count. We're talking about working from home or even on the fly in airports, conference centers, or client sites. The best virtual setup to me is working from home because it comes with the most advantages. Let's break down the upside and downside of such an arrangement.

The Upside

There are three primary advantages to setting up a home office versus commuting to work every day:

1. **The commute is eliminated.** During my days in corporate America, I technically lived fewer than 10 miles from my office. Unfortunately, thanks to traffic and congestion, those 10 miles took 90 minutes to drive. That's nine minutes per mile for those keeping score at home. Am I crazy, or could I walk at a quicker pace? Then again, do I really want to traverse the Lincoln Tunnel by foot?

   Right away the virtual office gives me back three hours per day. That's 15 hours per week thanks to a new commute that's just down the hall. Without even reviewing the other advantages, we've already reduced your working time considerably.

2. **Office distractions are reduced.** Try this experiment ... see how long it takes you to write a two-page memo from the office versus from home. Thanks to colleagues popping by your desk and unexpected meetings, a two-page memo can take all day. The end result is you fall behind on your other work and end up working late to catch up. The late night means more time spent at the office, not less.

   Crank out that memo from home, uninterrupted, and you'll be done in an hour or less. That leaves the rest of the day for the remaining work you want to get done. Who knows, you may even finish up early and catch that little league game with your boss.

3. **Out of sight, out of mind.** An urgent project comes up at 5:15 P.M. and your boss comes flying out of her office looking for an able pair of hands. Who do you think gets picked first, you sitting at home or your colleague 10 feet away in a cubicle? That's right … your unsuspecting colleague has to drop everything to put out the end-of-day fire. Meanwhile, you've shut down for the day and started playing Parcheesi with the family.

Okay, so maybe you're thinking this colleague scores brownie points for jumping in to help, but is that really how people get rated at year-end? Most employers go back to goals from January to see how you performed. I doubt fire-fighting was on the list of top priorities. So stay home and crank out the top deliverables that matter most and you'll be just fine.

Ask Jeff _____

Isn't there a connection between your boss seeing your face and getting promoted? While out of sight, out of mind prevents fire-fighting at the office, couldn't it also get you passed over for a raise? The answer is yes, and that's why you need to continue to show up for important meetings and keep your mug front and center in everyone's mind (even if you only show it three or four times per month).

The Downside

It's not all roses and candy canes when it comes to working from home, so here are two potential pitfalls to keep in mind. Floundering on either one can instantly sabotage your efforts to truly work fewer hours than before you went virtual.

1. **Office politics are replaced with "homework."** When I say "homework," I'm not referring to solving algebra problems to study for a pop quiz tomorrow morning. I mean those little house projects that can suck up your time quicker than a vacuum cleaner works in a Styrofoam factory. You're supposed to be in your home office cranking out work at 9 A.M. Instead you meet the plumber to fix a leak, run to the post office to mail a package, and sneak in a doctor's appointment.

Now don't get me wrong, the beauty of a virtual arrangement is you can squeeze in these little to-do's mid-week instead of all on Saturday. But if you go overboard with house projects, then you'll never achieve the goal of working less. Instead you'll be staying up past midnight to catch up on work time missed thanks to plumbers, mailmen, and doctors.

2. **Your work and life find little or no separation.** With a baby at home, playtime is only two rooms away. Sure we have a nanny, but who can resist the urge to at least hug your child every hour or so? Hey, I love the fact that I can see my son on a moment's notice. But I also recognize that if I've allotted two hours to work on a presentation, I can't spend 45 minutes playing peek-a-boo. For the virtual office to truly achieve a working-less atmosphere, you've got to clearly differentiate working versus nonworking time.

Jackpot Scenario 2: The Compressed Workweek

The virtual office is not the answer for everyone, particularly if you don't have a great setup at home. My second top choice for a flexible setup is the compressed workweek.

The Definition

How does a compressor work? Basically it crams more stuff into a smaller space than would be possible without mashing everything together. The compressed workweek follows the same model. Let's say you work 35 hours per week spread over five days. That's seven hours per day. In a compressed workweek you squeeze 35 hours per week into four days instead of five. So now you're working eight hours and forty-five minutes per day instead of seven hours. An alternative setup is to spread the compressed workweek over two weeks and squeeze ten days of work into nine days. In this model you get every other Friday off instead of every Friday.

Before you call me on the hotline to say 35 hours is still 35 hours, answer a simple question: Do you currently just work 9 to 5? Thanks to ever-increasing work pressure, most folks get in early and leave late already. When I worked in corporate America I regularly arrived at 8:30 A.M. and stayed until 6:30 or 7 P.M. When my team implemented a compressed workweek, my workday Monday through Thursday felt exactly the same. The big difference was instead of spending Friday in the office, I spent it on the golf course, running errands, or seeing a matinee for half price.

The Upside

Similar to the virtual office, let's lay out three advantages and two disadvantages to the compressed workweek. First, the upside:

1. **You own your Friday.** How much do you enjoy New Year's Day, July 4, and Labor Day? That extra day off makes the week more manageable. It can even make food taste better after eight or nine tough five-day workweeks in a row. The compressed workweek hands you three-day weekends every single week (or every other week if you spread the compression over two weeks). You just handed yourself that New Year's Day feeling every week of the year. Not a bad gig if you ask me.

2. **Your productivity improves.** There's something about working only four days in a week that forces you to get more done. You know you have limited time, so you focus and make progress. It's like if someone asked you to empty a dishwasher in five minutes versus five hours. With five minutes on the clock you'll dive right in and make it so. Given five hours you won't even start the task for an hour or two.

3. **People respect your Friday.** When you work five days per week, people paw at your time all day long, even into the evening. They know you're accessible all week so they have no qualms about asking for meetings morning, noon, and night throughout the week. But when you work on a compressed timetable, people slowly get the idea you're out of pocket on Fridays. Slowly but surely they stop asking for meetings that day and you really get that precious day for just you.

Ask Jeff

Will people who work five days per week really respect your Friday freedom? Won't they just be jealous and try to sabotage your extra day off? It's true compressed workweeks are best structured when the entire department follows this model. But you still can be successful alone by setting boundaries early and refusing to cave. Soon enough, colleagues will catch on to the new regime and stop bugging you on Friday.

The Downside

It's not all long weekends when it comes to the compressed workweek. Two potential pitfalls can lead to more working hours, not less.

1. **Failure to set boundaries on Fridays.** You crank out work over extended hours Monday through Thursday to earn your precious Friday. You're in the elevator at 7 P.M. Thursday, dreaming about freedom for the next three days. All of a sudden a colleague pops the elevator door open just before it shuts. He really needs your help on a big deliverable due Friday afternoon. Reluctantly you agree to help and kiss your extended weekend goodbye. Soon enough word spreads that you're available on Fridays, too. End-of-week work becomes the norm, and you lose the whole advantage of the compressed week.

2. **Working way too late Monday through Thursday.** Remember, the goal of this chapter is to work less, not more. So if you're staying until midnight Monday through Thursday just for a taste of Friday freedom, then you've missed the point of the compressed workweek. The idea is to focus and get your work done during normal business hours. You're not trying to work 60 hours in four days to fool yourself into thinking Friday off is really a working-less scenario.

Jackpot Scenario 3: The Extended Vacation

If the virtual office and compressed workweek don't suit your style, your third and final option is the extended vacation. If you can't work from home or squeeze five days into four, at least you can go for more than two weeks' vacation.

The Definition

Extended vacations are most typically packaged up as paid sabbaticals. You might have to work 5 or 10 years to qualify, but the idea is to leave your company for 3, 6, or 12 months and pursue a nonwork-related venture. It could be a charitable cause, a research project, or even a not-for-profit job. You keep your salary and benefits but get a completely different experience from your typical workday.

Some companies offer variations of paid sabbaticals such as mini-vacations. Here you might work nine months and then get three off to recharge your batteries. This setup is dependent on companies structured to support this model. There are of course various nonpaid mini-vacations you can take, but then you're working less and earning less. That runs counter to the point of this book, so let's leave that out for now.

The Upside

Scoring a paid sabbatical or other paid leave from work comes with upsides and downsides, just like the virtual office and compressed workweek. I'm sure you've caught the pattern by now ... three advantages and two disadvantages.

1. **You're really away from the office.** Three, six, or twelve months paid away from the office will really drive home the advantages of working less. It will take less than a week for the daily grind to melt away. Unlike a compressed workweek, your body will really feel recharged when the mini-vacation ends. It will bring back those memories of summer camp when you lollygagged through two full months of nonschool-related activities.

2. **It's a resumé builder.** You may not realize it, but nine years on the job plus one year in a unique experience makes for better interview fodder than 10 years on the job. If you eventually leave your current employer, you can wow your future boss with stories the typical interviewee never shares. Your new employer will appreciate the chance to hear about experiences other than cross-functional collaboration, analytical skills, and people leadership.

Less Is More

Can it really be true that less work experience is more valuable than more work experience? Absolutely, if the way you spent the nonworking time can be tied into personal growth. For example, if you worked with Doctors Without Borders for six months, you learned to help people and diagnose problems. Clearly, you can show how those skills would help on the job.

3. **You can bring the family along.** Why limit the mini-vacation to just you? Work it out so the whole family can experience time away from the workplace grind. It's a paid sabbatical, so money is no object. Remember, the whole goal of working less is to enjoy life more. So get your spouse and kids on board with the plan and build family relationships like never before. It will make up for those late nights when you missed the school play and parent/teacher conferences.

The Downside

It's not all piña coladas and cool sabbatical breezes when you land an extended vacation. You've got to look out for two potential problems.

1. **Will your job be there when you get back?** You've got to make sure your company holds your job or at the very least guarantees you a similar position when you return. The idea is to not sabbatical yourself right out of a job. So work out these details before you begin your mini-vacation, otherwise you might be in for a surprise on the back end.

2. **Can you overcome the perception of a slacker?** You might view your sabbatical as a once-in-a-lifetime opportunity to study marine life off the coast of Australia's Great Barrier Reef. Your boss may view it as shirking your responsibilities on the job. After all, you can't exactly crank out PowerPoint presentations underwater. Make sure your boss is really on board with this move and not approving it against his will. Otherwise you're in for a tough time when you return to the office.

The Least You Need to Know

◆ You can only work less and earn more in your current job if your role or company offers the flexibility to make it happen for you.

◆ People who underperform rarely earn the right to begin a flexible working arrangement, so start delivering big time.

◆ There's a right way to approach your boss to pitch a flexible arrangement that offers the highest likelihood of a positive response.

◆ Virtual offices, compressed workweeks, and mini-vacations are three of the best ways to work less and earn more without leaving your current job.

Chapter 5

Why Hire a Consultant When You Can Be One Yourself?

In This Chapter

- ♦ A systematic approach to quitting your job
- ♦ Uncovering insights from your career history
- ♦ Identifying your unique talents and strengths
- ♦ Rounding out your skill set to be more marketable
- ♦ Turning talent into a thriving consulting practice

A traditional corporate America job is your biggest obstacle to achieving a working-less, earning-more lifestyle. Depending on your career choice and industry, you're committing anywhere from 40 to 100 hours per week at the office.

With a fixed 168 hours available to you every week, you're spending anywhere from 25 to 60 percent of your precious hours at a desk, on the road, or in meetings. Throw in another

50 hours per week for sleep and up to 90 percent of your entire week is spoken for the moment your radio alarm plays "Working for the Weekend" at 6:05 A.M. Monday. Unless you want to start multitasking by eating in the shower or answering e-mails while changing diapers, you'll need to free up some time.

The natural answer is to either work less or sleep less. Given the choice of sacrificing work or sleep, I'll lose the work and keep the sleep thank you very much. Does that mean you should quit your job first thing tomorrow? Absolutely not! The key is to discover your personal expertise and leverage those skills to become a high-paid, in-demand consultant.

Being a Quitter Isn't Always a Bad Thing

Take a wild guess what my parents initially said when I informed them of my plans to quit a stable, six-figure job at American Express.

- We didn't send you to college to quit your job.

- How will you make any money without a steady paycheck?

- Will your boss give you your job back if you tell her you made a terrible mistake?

- If you're thinking of moving back home, it's too late … we already turned your old bedroom into a billiards room.

- All of the above.

To say my parents, close friends, and co-workers questioned the sanity of my decision would be a major understatement. Phrases like "you're crazy" and "good luck living as a starving artist" still ring in my ears. Let me be the first to tell you the road less traveled is less traveled for a reason. It takes courage and conviction to do something different from everyone around you. The doubters and naysayers always come out full-force to challenge your motives.

Rest assured most of this negativity is fueled by jealousy, ignorance, or fear and will dissipate the moment you achieve your first taste of success. In fact, most of the early naysayers now invite me to dinner to coach them on achieving the very lifestyle they first shunned. I figure a free dinner here and there makes up for the initial lack of support (especially when you order steak or the catch of the day).

Less Is More _____

As with any life-changing decision you'll be tempted to bounce your plans off family, friends, yoga instructor, the tollbooth collector, and anyone else who will listen. There's nothing wrong with confiding in a few trusted confidants, but limit the voices advising you. Otherwise you'll end up in a confused state of self-doubt, and that's a terrible way to undertake an exciting career transition.

The key to quitting your job successfully is to take a systematic approach. If I had made a rash decision to leave American Express, I would have wasted my degree, needed money, begged for my old job back, and apparently spent nights sleeping on a pool table.

Systematic Quitting—Part 1, Income Replacement

Confidence to quit your steady job comes from the realization you can replace, or even increase, your income through alternative means. In this chapter, we focus on achieving this goal through consulting.

Let's keep things simple and assume I forfeited an annual salary of $100,000. The goal is to replace or increase that salary through consulting revenue. The question becomes how much you'll need to charge and how many days you'll need to work to hit $100,000 or more in income. Let's look at two examples, one that entails maintaining your current income and the other increasing your income by 50 percent.

Determining Your Target Daily Consulting Rate: Example 1

Question	Answer
How much do you want to earn annually?	$100,000
How many days do you want to consult?	50 per year
Your daily consulting rate needs to be:	$2,000 per day

Notice you're now earning $100,000 annually working just one day per week for 50 weeks. That leaves two full weeks of vacation, plus another four days every single week to tone your biceps and glutes, read a *Harry Potter* book, or even watch your daughter smack a two-run double in an after-school softball match.

Does $2,000 per day for consulting seem unrealistic to you? Some consultants actually earn $5,000 or more per day, so shooting for $2,000 is within your reach. Later in this chapter, I'll show you exactly how to hit your target consulting rate.

Maybe your goal is to raise your income by 50 percent to $150,000 and you're willing to work four days per week to make it happen. After all, you really should be able to shape those biceps or tighten those glutes with three free days per week. Here's how you would calculate your daily consulting-rate target.

Determining Your Target Daily Consulting Rate: Example 2

Question	Answer
How much do you want to earn annually?	$150,000
How many days do you want to consult?	200 per year
Your daily consulting rate needs to be:	$750 per day

In this example, you're interested in working four days per week and your target income is $150,000. That takes the pressure off by $2,000 per day because you'll only need $750 to reach your annual-earnings target.

Fear Busters

Maintaining health coverage is a common concern for consultants working on their own. What will you do if you notice a suspicious mole? In a moment of honesty, most corporate climbers will tell you company health costs continue to get passed along to workers, wiping out a once valuable benefit. If you're married, consider getting coverage through your spouse's employer. If not, rest assured there are programs out there designed for sole proprietors to pool their medical needs into reasonably priced group coverage.

These two examples involve working fewer than five days each week while replacing or even increasing your income. Not a bad life compared to five days per week, 50 weeks per year in a cubicle listening to the person next to you on the phone debating a fantasy football trade all morning.

Systematic Quitting—Part 2, Consulting Expertise

Earning anywhere from $750 to $5,000 per day sounds great, but is anyone really going to pay you that fee for consulting? Sitting at my corporate America desk, I struggled with this very question. Who am I to demand $2,000 for the privilege of sitting next to me for a day? When you put it that way, fear emerges and you quickly dive back into the comfort and routine of checking e-mails, responding to voicemails, and googling your favorite celebrity during a lunch break.

The better question to ask yourself is what would it take for someone to jump at the chance to pay you $2,000 for a day? The answer is finding someone who believes the consulting value you'll provide outweighs the fee you charge. In other words, if you possess a specific expertise that can generate thousands of dollars for a client or save them significant time and energy, they'll gladly cough up $2,000 a day to learn what you already know. Examples might include:

- ◆ Implementing a new technology that can shave $250,000 annually off operating expenses.

- ◆ Writing a manual for a national sales team to double their odds of closing deals with new prospects.

- ◆ Completing accounting forms for a small business and saving it thousands of dollars through tax breaks.

- ◆ Teaching an aspiring architect how to design blueprints sure to land new business with customers.

- ◆ Improving a client's new product development process to increase revenue and speed up time to market.

Granted, you may know nothing about technology, freelance writing, sales training, accounting, or new product development. These are just examples. Don't worry; in the next section, we'll work together to discover your specific and marketable consulting expertise. It all comes down to looking into your past history to uncover those unique talents companies or individuals will pay top dollar to acquire.

Your Past Is the Key to Your Future

By now you're hopefully intrigued at the possibility of earning top dollar for your consulting expertise. You're hopefully even more intrigued at the possibility of doing it in fewer than five days per week. But how do you really figure out that unique expertise? The answer lies in your resumé, and I'm going to show you right now how to find that expertise. If you need a few extra minutes to dust off your resumé, I can wait. A working-less lifestyle allows me to be patient these days.

You might think this is a straightforward process. For example, if you've been an accountant for the last 20 years, shouldn't you quit your job and simply provide accounting consulting? In the late 1990s, I would have agreed with you. At the time, I was a marketing manager for American Express. When the idea of working less, earning more first hit me, I assumed I'd have to become a marketing consultant. A deeper look into my past revealed something quite different. I'd like to walk you through the very exercise that uncovered my true expertise and road to a thriving consulting practice.

Here are three simple steps that will change how you view both your career and your true area of expertise:

1. Write down the job titles of your last four positions.

2. Sum up in one sentence your primary responsibilities in each role.

3. Think back to your single favorite project from each of the four roles and write that project down.

To help you along, here's how I answered these three questions.

A Review of My Last Four Jobs

Job Title	Primary Role	Favorite Project
Business Consultant	Help clients manage T&E costs	Undergraduate recruiting

Job Title	Primary Role	Favorite Project
Senior Consultant	Research business	Employee satisfaction
	Travel trends and forecasts	Initiative
Marketing Manager	Develop promotions for Membership Rewards partners	Philanthropy project
Account Manager	Act as main contact for corporate card clients	Employee career planning and development

Now it's your turn. It doesn't matter if all four roles were at the same company or four different companies. Fill out the chart like I did and then we'll analyze it together.

🕐 **Time and a Half**

Do you need a shortcut to remember back to those last four jobs? Here's a quick tip to refresh your memory. Turn on your computer and pull up files that contain old resumés or even performance reviews. You'd be amazed how easy it is to forget entire jobs. Our minds are crammed with birthdays to remember, baseball statistics, celebrity gossip, and random to-do items, so sometimes you need some paper documentation to remember where you've been.

A Review of Your Last Four Jobs in Corporate America

Job Title	Primary Role	Favorite Project
1.		
2.		
3.		
4.		

My Aha Moment

The day I filled out this chart I stared in disbelief. How could my four favorite projects all fall under the human resources umbrella when my primary jobs called for marketing, promotions, and account management? Why did I keep gravitating toward these projects when they were nowhere in my job descriptions?

It turns out I had been repeatedly volunteering for these side projects without noticing the human resources theme. Something at a subconscious level drew me to undergraduate recruiting, employee satisfaction, charity projects, and career development.

Was I just procrastinating from my primary to-do items in favor of side projects? Not really. I thought back to my college days and it dawned on me I had completed a dual degree in marketing and psychology. As graduation approached, my sensible side directed me toward a marketing career. But I never lost sight of my passion for psychology, a love for the way people think and act.

The connection hit me faster than my newborn son puts anything you give him directly in his mouth. Recruiting new talent, striving for employee satisfaction, giving back to the community, and influencing employee careers all loosely fit together under my passion for psychology. This personal realization represented the very beginning of uncovering my true expertise. I immediately began asking myself additional questions:

- ◆ Why had I never noticed this trend of favorite projects before?

- ◆ How could I manage to do even less marketing and more human resources work to further explore this passion?

- ◆ Why did I put my psychology degree in storage when I should have hung it up on the wall as a reminder?

- ◆ Does the guy in the cubicle next to me think I'm strange for asking all these questions out loud?

Your Aha Moment

What about you? Take a close look at your primary roles and favorite projects on your worksheet. Do your favorite projects look and feel like your primary roles in each job? Or, like me, do you see for the first time a new trend? Your favorite projects represent what you truly enjoy doing at work, not what you are paid to do every day. You might like these projects so much you actually wish they could become your full-time job at work. If that's the case, then you're beginning to understand where your true expertise lies. It's not always what you're paid to do, it can often be those side projects that you keep gravitating toward.

Less Is More

Don't overthink this exercise. Human resources jumped out for me right away, and I'll bet some trends are hitting you like a hail storm in the Midwest. Don't ignore the obvious trends, themes, and takeaways. This is the time for straightforward thinking.

We explore this concept further in the next section, but in the meantime ask yourself these questions:

- Do your favorite projects or key skills have anything in common?

- Is there an industry, corporation, or department in your company where you could do more of these projects?

- Do these favorite projects remind you in any way of something you used to enjoy in college or growing up?

- Like me, should you apologize to the guy in the next cubicle for talking to yourself?

Your Consulting Profit Is in Your Favorite Projects

Discovering your favorite projects is enlightening, but the next obvious question is why you like these specific projects. For me, I realized I had a passion for human resources work, but why? For example, what drew me to undergraduate recruiting? Did I enjoy scouring college campuses for the next generation of talent? Or did I simply treasure sitting on the other side of the interview desk watching new recruits squirm, sweat, and fidget over tough questions like "How would you figure out the total number of bicycles in China?" By the way, if you're curious about

Chinese culture, I'd recommend *The Complete Idiot's Guide to Modern China* by Vanessa Lide Whitcomb and Michael Benson. It could be a fun read with all the free time you'll have after building a work-less, earn-more lifestyle.

As I delved further into this passion for human resources, I realized that projects in this area rarely felt like work. Human resources somehow energized and motivated me while my primary responsibilities left me drained, tired, and bored. So I asked myself an additional question about human resources. What did I enjoy most about these favorite projects? My results are shown in the following table.

My Favorite Work Within My Favorite Projects

Favorite Projects	Favorite Work Within Projects
Undergraduate recruiting	Writing job descriptions; presenting at colleges
Employee satisfaction initiative	Researching and writing about employee needs; presenting findings to senior management
Philanthropy project	The feeling of giving to and helping others; presenting results against goals at department town hall meetings
Employee career planning and development	Coaching employees to reach their potential and improve their leadership skills

As I analyzed my favorite projects within my favorite work, themes started to emerge. It became clear I enjoyed specific aspects of human resources, mainly …

♦ Writing and researching.

♦ Presenting in front of groups.

♦ Coaching and helping others.

Now I was getting somewhere. It was clear my real passion is for writing, presenting, and coaching in human resources and personal development. At this point I had no idea how to earn consulting dollars from this epiphany, but I was making tremendous progress. Remember, at the time I was sitting in my office with full-time responsibilities in marketing. I was both energized and terrified at my findings: energized by uncovering my true passion, but terrified by the prospect of reinventing the marketer I thought I would be when I graduated college.

Ask Jeff

While teaching these concepts in seminars I often hear the following: "My boss won't let me volunteer for projects outside my primary area of responsibility. As much as I want to gain new and varied experience, my boss keeps me stifled."

There's a word for these kinds of bosses: blockers. These are bosses whose only concern is pigeon-holing you into producing for just them. Any attempt to better yourself is seen as a direct threat to their leadership. Simply put, you've got to get out from under a blocker's leadership or you'll have to work that much harder to implement the strategies in this book.

The next three sections of this chapter will break down exactly how my passion for human resources turned into actual consulting profit. But first we've got to find out what you like most about those favorite projects, so grab a pen.

Your Favorite Work Within Your Favorite Projects

Favorite Projects	Favorite Work Within Projects
1.	
2.	
3.	
4.	

Fear Busters

If you're like me, you may be realizing you've spent years working in the wrong industry, the wrong type of work, and the wrong projects, and potentially playing away from your strengths. It's exciting to gain self-insight but also scary to realize you may need to change course to reach your potential. Look at it this way … changing now is scary, but doing nothing will lead to more years in the wrong situation and a lifetime of regret.

Now go one step further and look for themes in your favorite work. Remember how I liked writing, presenting, and coaching within the human resources industry? What themes emerge for you as you analyze your work? Take your time here because this really is the key to building a profitable consulting practice.

Why is it so important to build a consulting business based on these findings? I'll give you four reasons. Why four? Well, most people stop their lists at three, so consider this a free bonus that will hopefully convince you to go for it:

1. The more you enjoy your work, the less it will feel like work, and that makes earning money more pleasurable.

2. You'll be playing to your strengths, meaning you'll be better than many of your competitors in the field.

3. When you enjoy your work and play to your strengths, you work faster, and this book is all about working less.

4. All of the above. Okay, so that shouldn't count as a real fourth reason, and I promised four legitimate reasons. How about the fact that many successful entrepreneurs will tell you their earnings really took off when they focused on their passions, strengths, and natural talents? So build a business around what you're good at and you'll naturally work less and earn more.

At this point, you know the industry you like, the projects in that industry, and the specific kind of work that suits you best. The next natural question is how to build your skill set around the work you like to build a marketable consulting practice.

Bolstering Your Skill Set Around What You Enjoy

We're now at the moment that either excites or scares most people. There's excitement because you can see, maybe for the first time, an avenue to making money doing something you enjoy. However, there's also fear because you may not resemble that person today. How will you ever reinvent yourself and become marketable to others?

The good news is that there are already plenty of folks who are very successful in the very field you want to enter. So rather than start from scratch, it becomes all about modeling the behavior of someone else. Following an already charted path is so much easier than creating one yourself. Just ask Lewis and Clark, who would have navigated the Pacific Northwest much quicker had roads and navigation systems been invented already.

 Time and a Half

Bolstering your resumé can be a scary proposition. Unlike a straight-forward check-off, say paying the bills or emptying the dishwasher, this one requires more thought and several mini-to-do items. The key to jumping into action is to break down the larger task into several smaller, more manageable to-do's. Think of it like planning a wedding. Rather than waking up every day saying you have to plan a wedding, it's better to break it down into tasks needed six months out, three months out, and so on.

You Don't Have to Be Lewis and Clark to Explore

So how do you reinvent yourself as a marketable consultant who can command top dollar in fewer hours? It comes down to answering three simple questions:

♦ What are the skills possessed by someone who would be well qualified as a consultant in your desired area?

♦ Which of those skills do you currently possess?

♦ What steps could you take to close the gap on the missing skills?

When I realized I wanted to become a writer, presenter, and coach in the field of human resources, I answered these very same questions.

Ideas to Build My Consulting Practice

Profile Needed	Do I Have It?	Steps to Close the Gap
Certification or Degree in HR	No	Choose program and submit application

continues

Ideas to Build My Consulting Practice (continued)

Profile Needed	Do I Have It?	Steps to Close the Gap
Grow skills in human resources	No	Get mentored by HR exec to build skill set
Active in speaking, writing industry	No	Research organizations, clubs, and magazines and join as appropriate
Corporate clients willing to pay for my services	No	Build Rolodex of clients and learn from already successful consultants

My focus shifted from fear to motivation as I broke down what it would really take to transform myself into a marketable consultant. Certainly I could get HR certified, continue volunteering for HR projects, be-come active in speaking and writing organizations, and learn what it takes to build a Rolodex of active clients. Would this task be as easy as ordering a pepperoni pizza for dinner? No. Would it be as difficult as I initially thought when I embarked on this journey? Another no.

These baby steps in the right direction generated the positive momentum to make the transformation complete, and I know you can do the same.

So what about you? What would it take to build a profile that could turn you into a marketable consultant?

Ideas to Build Your Consulting Practice

Profile Needed	Do You Have It?	Steps to Close Gap
1.	Yes or No?	1.
		2.
		3.
2.	Yes or No?	1.
		2.
		3.

Profile Needed	Do You Have It?	Steps to Close Gap
3.	Yes or No?	1.
		2.
		3.
4.	Yes or No?	1.
		2.
		3.

Nine Strategies to Navigate Your Success

You've got the action plan to reinvent yourself as a marketable consultant. But what are some of the less tangible steps you can take to move in the right direction? I'm glad I asked because it just so happens I have a handy-dandy list of nine strategies to navigate your success beyond your action plan. Remember, the goal is to start building credentials in the industry you desire and projects you want as a consultant. Keep that in mind as we go through the list.

Ask Jeff _____

Here's a common question I hear: "With a spouse and kids isn't it safer to just stay where I am rather than risk everything on a new path?" Hey, I understand this fear as someone who walked this very line. I always give the same advice. If you can make peace with your current job and career and won't have regrets, stay. If you're going to feel uneasy and itching to change for the next 30 years, you've got to take action. Plus, this is not a get-rich-quick scheme; it's a methodical plan to reinvent yourself.

1. Find a mentor: successful people love to mentor inexperienced folks starting out.

2. Volunteer for opportunities: keep an open ear for opportunities in your chosen area and go for it.

3. Connect with influential leaders: it's amazing how knowing the right person can sometimes make all the difference.

4. Suggest a new project: don't wait for opportunities, proactively suggest a project to build your skill set.

5. Be helpful and resourceful: if you know peers in your desired industry, help them out and they'll think highly of you.

6. Perform at the next level: don't wait for a promotion to gain experience at the next level, act that way today.

7. Demonstrate your expertise: maybe your boss doesn't even know about your hidden talents.

8. Get involved in the industry: join organizations that can expose you to successful people in the right industry.

9. Enjoy the ride: remember, when you love your work it should feel energizing. If it doesn't, recheck your approach.

Now we're really cooking. But the obvious next question is how you really start making money in less time. After all, this isn't *The Complete Idiot's Guide to Hobby Discovery*. So let's get into what it takes to turn this marketable consulting expertise into some greenbacks.

Turning Your Favorite Projects into Income

There is one question people always ask me about the jump from corporate America to a profitable consulting business. How do you actually make the leap? That's the scary part and that's what often stops folks in their tracks before they give it a real shot. Having stared fear in the face and gone for it, I've boiled the process down to five straightforward steps. Follow the steps and hopefully the fear melts away quicker than a snow cone sitting on the equator.

Step 1: Do the Exercises Like You Mean It

So the last few sections of this book asked you to complete some introspective exercises. You've got three choices whenever you come across exercises in a book:

♦ Passively read the exercises and say to yourself, "Interesting stuff, but who has time to write in a book?"

♦ Actively complete the exercises and say to yourself, "I'm finally going to take charge of my career!"

♦ Rip out the exercises, use them as kindling in your fireplace, and say to yourself, "I just saved money on logs."

Believe it or not, I view choices one and three as equal. Passively reading exercises is nearly identical to crumpling them up for kindling. So if you just skimmed the last few sections, go back and take the time to complete the exercises like you mean it.

 Time and a Half

If you're struggling to find the motivation to get started on the exercises, I have a simple solution. Start with the least intimidating exercise first. Do them out of order if you have to. Just pick something that scares you the least and put pen to paper. Then pick the second least scary exercise.

Step 2: Assess Your Current Work Environment

Once you truly know the industry and project work you enjoy most, it's time to honestly assess your work environment. Are you employed by someone who can help you get where you need to go? For example, my company was large enough that I could systematically maneuver from the marketing department to human resources. I also had a boss who supported my journey toward career self-discovery.

What about your company? Can you make the move to a department more in line with your consulting desires? Do you work for a supportive boss or a blocker? In essence, you're in one of two scenarios:

♦ Scenario One: the opportunity exists for you to systematically acquire the business skills you'll need to become a marketable and profitable consultant.

♦ Scenario Two: your company, department, or boss is blocking you from acquiring the business skills you'll need to become a marketable and profitable consultant.

If you're in Scenario One, then it's all systems go. You've got the game plan from the previous sections and it's all about taking action and making it so. If you're in Scenario Two, the road is somewhat more difficult and you've got to ask yourself three critical questions:

- Is there a way to work for a different boss in this or another department to acquire the skills I need?

- Is there a way to change departments so I can acquire the skills I need?

- Do I need to change companies in order to acquire the skills I need?

As you can imagine, these three questions are listed in order from easiest to toughest fix. But if you don't face these tough questions, then you're simply settling for your unfortunate circumstances. That's no way to take charge of your career and no way to ultimately work less while earning more.

Step 3: Build Experience in Your Consulting Field

If you're not blocked by your boss, department, or company, then the only remaining obstacle is you. So get out of your own way and start building the skills you need. Remember the table I showed you of skills I needed to build my consulting practice:

- Choosing a program to apply for an advanced degree or certification in human resources.

- Landing an HR position or building HR skills to officially make the transition away from marketing.

- Researching organizations and clubs to become active in the speaking and writing industry.

- Building a Rolodex of potential consulting clients and learning from successful clients who have built profitable practices.

What about you? Go back to that action plan and start jumping into building that skill set.

Step 4: Consult to Your Employer First

I remember my senior year of college. I went to a bunch of interviews and heard the same comment from potential employers: "You seem like a bright guy but we're looking for someone with more experience."

This is the quandary any first-time employee faces. How can you have experience when it's your first job? That's like asking me to untie my shoes when I'm only wearing socks.

Landing that first consulting client has a similar feel. Established firms roll out the laundry list of impressive clients and use that list to sell new clients. All you've got is a business card and a dream. That's not enough to land a client. That's why I negotiated first with my current employer and landed them as my very first client.

I know what you're thinking ... why would your employer let you walk away from the company and then hire you back as a consultant after you just left them? It's all in how you position the situation to your boss. I made four things clear to my boss when I tried to arrange this setup:

1. I'm not leaving to go to a competitor just for the sake of making more money.

2. I'm happy to consult back to this department, particularly while you search for my replacement.

3. I want to give this consulting thing a shot but I would cherish the opportunity to return to work here if I fall flat on my face.

4. I've never worked for a more supportive boss and that's why I know you'll understand my long-term career dream.

These four points serve some very important roles. First, by making it clear you're not going to a competitor you come across as anything but money hungry. Second, by offering to pitch in while your replacement is found you come across as helpful. Third, you're complimenting your company. Finally, you're making your boss feel loved and that's always a smart move.

Step 5: Leverage Your Employer to Land Bigger Fish

The moment I scored a four-month consulting gig with my employer, I went into heavy sales mode. I viewed these four months as my monetary cushion to land the next big fish and I planned to drop my first client's name (i.e., my former employer) as often as possible to help me score that next client.

Less Is More

I actually wasted my first month creating the perfect sales brochure for potential clients. I realized that those first clients actually come from networking (i.e., who you know). These folks are not interested in your brochure skills. Rather, they're hiring you because of knowing you or because someone they trust vouched for you. So focus on networking and the Rolodex first, and brochure making down the road.

This is not the time to spend all of your days and nights building your website or creating overly elaborate business cards. You've got to sell, sell, sell. I used these four months to build my Rolodex, network, and ask anyone I could think of for consulting leads. To be honest, I found this exercise rather uncomfortable. I'm not a sales guy by nature. But I knew this was my chance to build a pipeline of prospects. I of course met much rejection, but by month three I had landed two new clients and was off and running.

Hitting the Bull's-Eye on Your Time and Revenue Targets

I'll be the first to admit that landing those first few clients is the toughest challenge you'll face. It really is what separates this venture from a hobby versus a fully functioning consulting practice. For the first few clients I really didn't worry about the hours I would have to work or the money they would pay me. The goal was simply to build confidence and prove to myself I could get paid for my expertise.

Once you get that initial jolt of confidence, it's time to turn your attention to the focus of this book ... working less and earning more. Do you remember earlier in this chapter when we talked about calculating your target consulting rate? You can flip back to that section or I can save you time with a quick reminder right here. There are two simple questions you have to ask yourself:

- How much do you want to earn annually?

- How many days do you want to consult?

If the goal is $100,000 per year and 50 consulting days per year (or two days per week), your target consulting rate is $2,000 per day. For my first three clients I was working more than 50 days per year and earning less than $2,000 per day. Like I said, the goal at the beginning is to land a few clients to build confidence and build that Rolodex of satisfied customers.

Ask Jeff

So how do you really determine the right consulting rate for you? As a rule of thumb, I suggest trying to duplicate your income in half the time. So if you were earning $50,000 per year in a full-time corporate job, see whether you can match that income in half the time. In this case that means working two and a half days per week for 50 weeks at a rate of $400 per day. Right away you would be working half the time and earning the same. If you want to truly earn more in less time, then shoot for $600 or $800 per day.

Now the focus needs to change to working less and earning more. With three clients underway you can afford to be more picky. I started brainstorming the kind of projects that would meet my criteria and came up with the following:

♦ Bigger companies tend to have bigger budgets and are usually used to spending $2,000+ per day for consultants.

♦ Projects that need to be completed in a short time tend to require more than two days of consulting per week.

♦ Working virtually most of the time for clients lends itself to a better work/life balance and more productive working hours (versus commuting hours).

With these three criteria in mind I built the profile of the ideal client. I wanted a bigger company with the luxury of time who didn't need to see me every day for a job well done. This specific profile helped me learn to say "no" to clients who didn't fit the bill. This is a hard concept to grasp at first. Potential clients would want to hire me but the rate would be too low or the project would be too demanding or I'd have to be onsite all the time. Yes, I wanted to make money, but I really stayed true to working less and earning more.

Did I think I was crazy the first time I turned down work after building up those first few clients? Yes, and so did my family, friends, former colleagues, bowling buddies, and the toll booth collector. I switched to E-Z Pass, by the way, to rid the negative toll booth collector from my life.

> **Fear Busters** _____
>
> Plenty has been written about the law of attraction. Basically it says that your thoughts lead to your actions, which lead to the results you want in life. Whether or not you believe in this law, I can tell you that negative thoughts will sabotage your effort. If you believe that no clients exist who meet your desired profile, you'll discourage yourself before your journey begins. Instead, believe those clients exist, because they do, and soon enough they'll be knocking on your door.

But guess what happened? After turning down projects outside my criteria, it cleared my mind and calendar to accept the right clients. In fact, if I had jumped at the wrong client just to make money, it likely would have cost me the right client later on because my plate would have been too full.

As you build the criteria for the perfect client, you, too, will at first be scared to say "no" to the wrong client. But you'll also find that this very specific criteria gives you a laserlike focus on finding those diamonds in the rough. So don't be afraid of the word "no," because it will make "yes" that much sweeter down the road.

The Least You Need to Know

♦ Quitting your job tomorrow is a recipe for failure. Systematically quitting your job is a recipe for success.

♦ Uncovering your unique expertise is the key to becoming a high-paid, in-demand consultant.

♦ You'll make more money in less time if you develop an expertise you actually enjoy doing.

♦ The easiest first consulting client to land is your current employer.

Chapter 6

Freelance Begins with the Word "Free"

In This Chapter

♦ The difference between freelancers and starving artists

♦ How freelance success depends as much on whom you know as what you know

♦ Why the Internet just might be the best invention for free-lancers looking to get the word out about their services

♦ The importance of joining freelance associations to land more business

♦ How to build a freelance pipeline that will keep new business rolling in for years to come

Just because "freelance" begins with the word "free" doesn't mean you're planning to work for peanuts. Quite the contrary, there's a huge difference between starving artists and freelancers. The starving artist makes little to no money hoping for a huge break that catapults him to stardom. The freelancer starts making money right away while building a steady stream of clients who desire her services. After client loyalty is established, you're on the way to a working-less, earning-more lifestyle.

In this chapter, I cover three primary strategies for building a successful freelance business. You learn the importance of relationship building so others can help prospect for you. You read about some of the best online sites that match up freelancers with those in need of work. I then talk about how industry associations can help shorten the cycle time it takes to find and sell-in new business.

I close by putting it all together so you can build a sustainable freelance business, one that keeps the dollars rolling in without working late nights and weekends. Freelance income continues to be one of my primary sources of revenue and I know it can be for you, too.

Debunking the Myths of Freelance Work

You're sitting at dinner with acquaintances when the inevitable "what do you do for a living" question comes up. After the typical lawyer, doctor, teacher, personal trainer responses, someone throws a curveball and says, "I'm a freelancer." Everyone nods and smiles warmly, but they're really thinking the following:

- "This guy clearly got fired from his job."
- "This guy is back home living with his parents."
- "This guy could make more money flipping burgers."
- All of the above.

I have no idea why freelancing is associated with unemployment, living with your parents, and burger flipping. My best guess is that most people criticize what they don't understand. Because freelancing sounds like the opposite of corporate America, folks choose to mock it. All I know is that after those mocking comments fade, the criticizers go back to their dreary jobs while the successful freelancers enjoy working less and earning more.

It's time once and for all to put to rest the misconceptions and misunderstandings associated with freelancing. Here's my top 10 list of the biggest myths out there.

Myth 1: Freelancing Is Another Word for Unemployed

Okay, I admit it. I do know some friends who became freelancers against their will. Thanks to ill-timed reorganizations and job cuts, their jobs went bye-bye. With insufficient time to land a new job, they passed the time as freelance contractors. When asked about their job search, they'd say "I'm freelancing while I search for my next corporate job."

Somehow this scenario became the universal explanation of why someone chooses to freelance. In reality, there are plenty of folks who make an informed decision to leave behind corporate jobs and get paid for their freelance efforts. Choosing to quit your job is not synonymous with unemployment; it's synonymous with a career change.

When I worked in corporate America I hired freelancers all the time, including writers, designers, media experts, technology whizzes, and even event planners. Not once did I ask whether these folks came straight from the unemployment line. In fact, watching them crank out their work without corporate bureaucracy and politics made me all the more curious to follow their path.

Myth 2: Freelancing at Home Kills Productivity

You tell people you're working from home and they confuse it with a day off. The next thing you know someone is asking you for a ride to the airport or the cable guy is coming to install wireless broadband Internet access. What should have been a day of freelance income generation is instead occupied with personal shuttle services and technology upgrades.

It is true that the house represents a potential vacuum of distractions. The television begs you to check out the latest episode of your favorite sitcom. A pile of laundry stares at you, hoping for a chance to get clean in the washing machine. Spouses, siblings, friends, and parents take advantage of your flexible schedule and start asking for favors.

This does not mean freelancing at home ruins productivity. It means you need to set boundaries. It took me some time to view my home office as somehow detached from my home life. But I've since mastered the difference between being home and working from home. One includes distractions and errands; the other is a great way to get work done without commutes.

Less Is More _____

I initially made the mistake of keeping nonbusiness-related stuff in my office. For example, my camcorder and charger sat just 2 feet from my desk. You catch the camcorder out of the corner of your eye and suddenly you're editing last month's vacation footage. The fewer nonwork-related distractions you keep in your office, the more work you'll get done. Check out www.WorkSpaces.com if you really want to design your space right.

Myth 3: Freelance Income Is Not Reliable

Twenty-six paychecks. That's the supposed guarantee of a corporate job if you get paid biweekly. My old boss used to call it a "gimme" because no matter how you performed, you could count on your direct deposit every other Friday. Switch to freelancing and your income supposedly becomes as reliable as getting a tan at midnight.

Do freelancers typically earn 26 biweekly paychecks? Probably not. Does that mean freelance income is unreliable? Not really. I worked with one client who paid me monthly for nearly three years. Another signed me to a one-year contract with the option to renew each year. The point is you can achieve reliable, consistent freelance income if you find the right clients.

More importantly, is that corporate paycheck really a "gimme," or could it be snatched away quicker than the last chocolate-covered strawberry on a dessert plate? People who have been fired will tell you one bad performance review, one new boss, or one downsizing is all it takes to convert your paycheck into a pink slip.

Myth 4: Freelancers Often Work Below Their Asking Price

Thanks to bidding wars, two freelancers can low-ball each other right out of a profitable project. What started as a $5,000 bid drops to $500 plus a 25 percent discount for paying on time. Or sometimes a freelancer might fear rejection so much he drops to a price point where even the stingiest client can't say "no."

Bidding wars and fearful freelancers are a fact of life, but neither has to drive how you do business. Earlier in this book, we talked about setting revenue targets. That means having the courage to say "no" to unprofitable or below-target gigs. Otherwise you're just confusing busyness with income.

As I've said before, it's okay to say "yes" at the beginning just to build a client base and pad your experience. After all, I earned just $75 for my first freelance job. But once you build confidence, it's time to say "no" to the wrong projects to open the door for the right projects.

Myth 5: Only Writers Qualify as Freelancers

"Freelance writer" is of course a popular phrase, and much of my freelance income has been derived from writing books, blogs, and articles. But writing is not the only way I've earned freelance income. Other channels include …

- Coaching clients one-on-one to improve their dating and relationship results.

- Creating a series of PowerPoint presentations for a busy executive including graphics and sound clips.

- Delivering a seminar on how to take charge of your career at an adult education school.

So if writing is your thing, by all means crank out the freelance books, blogs, and articles. There's room for everyone. But if you're allergic to putting pen to paper, you still can swim in the freelance pool anytime.

Myth 6: Freelancers Have to Work Around the Clock

Have I ever stayed up until midnight or later putting the finishing touches on a freelance project? Absolutely. Did I ever burn the midnight oil in the corporate world? Absolutely. Working late is not a function of corporate versus freelance income. It depends on whether or not you work for demanding clients and just how efficiently you can work.

Demanding clients aren't biased against freelancers. They'll call anyone at 5 P.M. on a Friday and insist on seeing results by 9 A.M. Monday. Procrastination is also not a term reserved for freelancers. Anyone can twiddle their thumbs for six hours before diving into the real work.

I tackle demanding clients by refusing to work for them a second time unless they change their ways. Does that seem like a risky proposition? Not when you consider that one demanding client can single-handedly ruin your working-less goals. As for procrastination, I put the freelance work at the top of my to-do list to make sure it gets done before the day slips away.

Myth 7: Freelancers Never Have Medical Benefits

I hear the medical benefits story all the time. "You can't leave corporate America! You'll lose your benefits, something terrible will happen, and you won't be covered." It is true that a major medical illness can wipe out an uninsured patient in no time. It is not true that medical benefits are offered only through large corporations.

Plus, I would hypothesize that if I asked 10 corporate employees how much they pay annually for medical coverage, at least 7 out of 10 would have no idea without scanning their pay stubs and running some numbers. Corporations have continued to cut down on medical coverage, pushing more and more health expenses to the employee. This means your precious coverage might not be the invaluable benefit you once believed.

I was shocked to find out that working as a sole proprietor I could receive the same medical benefits from my corporate days for just $150 extra per month. Is $1,800 per year really a big-enough expense to never risk leaving a corporate job for a chance at freelance freedom? Not in my book!

Myth 8: Freelancers Are Destined for Solitary Lives

Freelancers have been called everything from hermits to recluses. It's like once you commit to a freelance lifestyle you've inadvertently signed up for a life of loneliness and isolation.

You can choose to be a freelance writer who lives in a secluded cabin in West Virginia, with your only person-to-person interaction being the person delivering your mail. But you also can be a freelancer who thrives on teamwork and collaboration to get the job done. This book, for example, has required continuous interaction with an agent, editor, and designer. Freelance event planners can't plan a single wedding or bar mitzvah without relying on caterers, musicians, florists, and photographers.

So if you're an outgoing extrovert who thrives on personal contact, rest assured you can freelance without giving up your interactive ways. You just need to pick the projects that will force you out of the West Virginia cabin and into team-oriented projects.

Myth 9: Freelancers Have No Protection If They Get Sued

You make a mistake at work and the company has got your back. Make the same mistake as a freelancer and it costs you your house, car, and firstborn child. Lack of protection as a freelancer is a myth that can be solved through one conversation with an accountant.

My accountant encouraged me to setup a DBA, or Doing Business As, to establish myself as a business entity. My DBA, called Bold Road, has separate checking accounts and business credit cards that keep personal and business expenses separate. If something goes wrong on the job, it's my business on the line, not my personal life.

There are many choices when it comes to structuring a business. You can go with S-Corporations, partnerships, LLCs, or a host of customized options for the business you run. Take the time to let an expert guide you, and you'll mitigate the personal risk associated with lawsuits.

Myth 10: Freelance Income Can't Compete with a Salary

So maybe you can make a few bucks as a freelancer, but you'll never match that six-figure salary you left behind in corporate America. You'll end up crawling back to work once you fall behind on those mortgage payments. That's what a jealous corporate climber would want an aspiring freelancer to believe.

Sure I started with a $75 resumé gig, and I'd have to write over 1,300 resumés to hit the $100,000 mark. That's three-and-a-half resumés per day if I worked 365 days per year. That doesn't sound anything like working less and earning more.

The reality is it might take time to match your corporate income, but eventually you can surpass it. Unlike your old salary, which grew probably 3 to 4 percent each year, freelance income is not capped. You earn what people are willing to pay. I quickly found out that the right clients and the right projects add up to far more than a corporate salary could ever offer.

Freelance Strategy 1: Building Power Relationships

Do you remember that network of over 1,000 people we built in Chapter 3?

I'll save you the time by reminding you of the five-step plan to build a network of over 1,000 people in less than one week:

1. Get clear on the help you need.

2. Make a list of everyone you know.

3. Ask everyone you know who they know.

4. Join one relevant industry association.

5. Join one online networking or prospecting site.

These 1,000 people in your network form the foundation of what will become your power relationships. These are the people who can significantly improve your odds of scoring lucrative freelance gigs. Power relationships help open doors for you, connect you to new people, and leap-frog your business momentum. If you were choosing groomsmen or bridesmaids for your wedding and couldn't pick any friends or family, your power relationships could step right in for you.

The time has come for a one-question pop quiz. Of the 1,000 people in my network, how many do you believe I consider power relationships?

Choice A: All 1,000 people

Choice B: Somewhere between 300 and 500 people

Choice C: Somewhere between 50 and 100 people

Choice D: Fewer than 5 people

If you believe the answer is "A," you're not headed toward working less. It will take you the entire year just to talk to each of the 1,000 people, let alone build power relationships. If you chose "B," it will take you half a year to call everyone. This still falls in the overworking category. Choice "C" might be reasonable, but it's more likely you would build a network of 50 to 100 acquaintances, not power relationships.

The correct answer is "D." That's right—of the 1,000 folks I network with, I count only four among my power relationships. Believe it or not, these four people are responsible for more than 95 percent of my freelance income. I cherish these four relationships because these folks helped me land my book deals, online writing assignments, blog gigs, and presentations. Sure I'd love to believe these wonderful jobs came solely through my own personal drive, ambition, and sweat. But the reality is …

> **Fear Busters**
>
> I'm the first to understand if networking makes you a bit queasy. Don't forget I'm an introvert. If the thought of calling people instantly brings out the sweat beads, I highly recommend e-mail communication. You can plan exactly what you want to write, personalize the note, and only jump to live chatting if the e-mail receives a positive response.

- One man connected me to the agent looking for an author to write *The Complete Idiot's Guide to Working Less, Earning More*.

- One woman who worked at a company looking for a new dating and relationship writer notified me of the opening.

- One man introduced me to the head of content for a major online dating site and recommended me as a new writer.

- One woman opened the door for me to present "Take Charge of Your Career and Take Charge of Your Love Life" in the tri-state area.

So these four individuals together guided me, helped me, and opened doors for me to earn 95 percent of my freelance income. The other 996 people collectively are responsible for the remaining 5 percent of revenue. It's no wonder I cherish these four relationships like my closest friends and family.

I know what you're thinking: Why put all your eggs in these four baskets? Shouldn't you diversify your freelance portfolio and count on 8, 10, or 20 people? First off, keep in mind these power relationships can change over time. These four folks are not locked in for life. They represent the most important people in my network at this stage of my freelance career. Over time people swap in and out as circumstances and assignments change.

More importantly, allow me to share three reasons I've come to learn it's a mistake to build so many power relationships:

- **It's too time-consuming.** There's a reason most people have only two or three truly close friends. It's simply too much work and too time-consuming to develop so many deep-routed relationships. The same holds in making freelance connections. If you try to get too close to everyone, you end up close to nobody.

- **Growing relationships is easier than starting new ones.** Ask a salesperson whether it's easier to resell a product to an existing customer or prospect for new business. Every salesperson knows the key to success is to find a handful of loyal clients and resell to them over and over again. The same holds true for power relationships. It's easier to grow your current relationships than fish for new people to meet.

- **Comfort is king.** When someone knows you really well, they're more likely to keep you top of mind, think of you for assignments, and connect you with others who can help. This comfort factor is not to be underrated. Contacting someone once per year will simply not drive the same results as building a comfortable, close relationship with fewer people.

So if you're sold now on limiting the power relationships in your life, how exactly do you find those four magical people from a cast of 1,000? Isn't that like looking for a freelance needle in a haystack?

I'll admit the task of narrowing 1,000 people to four feels overwhelming at first. But I'm going to eliminate those fears right now by laying out exactly how I uncovered the right power relationships for my freelance career. Picture a huge funnel. You're going to pour those 1,000 people into the funnel (not literally of course ... I don't want anyone getting hurt). The funnel gets progressively narrower as fewer folks fit through until just the four power relationships emerge on the other side.

Okay, so there's a bit more to it than that, but I wanted to put the visual in your head. Now, here are the five steps I followed to pour the 1,000 through the funnel and identify my four power relationships.

Step 1: Reach Out to All 1,000 People

The holidays are a great time to kick off communication with your 1,000 people. Sure you can send a stock photo, but that doesn't quite get the bang for the buck. I recommend writing a form letter or e-mail that explains what you're up to. Remember, you're not actively asking for help at this stage, just letting people know you're a freelance writer, event planner, or whatever the case may be.

 Time and a Half _____

Does the thought of 1,000 notes give you writer's cramp? I find you can cut writing time dramatically by customizing the first paragraph and then using a stock note the rest of the way. Folks will see right away you've personalized the typed note and likely give you a free pass the rest of the way. Just be sure the opening paragraph is truly personal and shows you really know the note recipient.

Step 2: Research the 1,000 People

After the 1,000 notes are out the door, start researching the people on your list. Who do they work for? Who do they know? What experiences could they share with you? You're looking for the connection between the person and what you're trying to achieve as a freelancer. For example, someone who works at an online-dating site should set off lightning bolts in your mind if you're looking to write online dating content. The goal is to identify about 50 folks from the 1,000 who seem like they could be most helpful.

Step 3: Start Building Off the Hits

Let's say 50 of the 1,000 people write back to your note. Now you've got 100 good leads, the 50 who just wrote back plus the 50 from step two who seem like they could be most helpful. Hopefully you have some double dippers, too. These would be people on both lists of 50.

You identified them as helpful and they wrote back. Those are your burning-hot leads; they took the time to write back and you already know of a reason they could be helpful to your freelance career.

Step 4: Make Yourself Helpful

Here's where many people falter in their quest to build power relationships. Instead of relationship-building at this juncture, they jump right into asking for help. That approach is backward. First you want to be helpful to your hot leads. Remember, you've got this list of 100 now that seem like the best of the 1,000. Now you want to handpick the top 10 or 20 and call them up, ask them to lunch, or get together for a sporting event. Use this time to see what's keeping them up at night and find a way to solve their problems. If you do this successfully, these folks will be more than ready to return the favor and help you in the future. Remember, these lunches are tax-deductible as business expenses, so your wallet won't feel too bad a hit.

Step 5: Start Small and Build over Time

There will come a moment when you'll hear, "Thanks for helping me out. Let me know if I can ever do anything for you." This is your chance to lay it on the line. Don't ask for the moon, just something small like a connection to someone they know or a recommendation letter for a job opening. Now you've got a give-and-take relationship going. You can foster that relationship over time, continue to help each other, and sooner or later you'll have a power relationship on your hands.

Freelance Strategy 2: Generating Profitable Online Leads

Power relationships are important, but the Internet can be your best friend, too. In fact, if I were planning a wedding today, I'd make power relationships and the Internet my co–best men.

When it comes to scoring lucrative freelance gigs, sites abound that can match your skill set to available freelance projects. Think of it like online dating, but instead of searching for your soul mate you're in the market for freelance gigs. I've had much success bringing in new business through the various sites out there.

What follows are my recommendations for the top 10 freelance sites around. For each I'll describe how it works plus what I like about the given site. You can pick and choose from the list, check them out, and be on your way to landing freelance gigs from the comfort of your home office. I don't get commissions or kickbacks from the sites for my recommendations, so rest assured these are objective analyses of what's out there.

Site 1: www.Guru.com

How it works: With more than 5,000 projects in over 150 categories at any one time, there's something for everyone at Guru.com. My most lucrative online freelance gig came through this site, and that's why I rate it number one. All you have to do is post your resumé and begin searching for open projects. Guru.com will even send you openings that match your freelance experience. You can stick with a no-fee membership or pay a small fee to become a featured freelancer and gain access to projects before they hit the nonpaying members. Don't worry if a few lowball projects come your way at first. Stick with it and eventually the gems will emerge.

What I like: Guru.com offers a two-way search feature. First, you can search all open projects and apply to any that seem like a good fit. Second, Guru.com will automatically notify you if a potential employer reviewed your qualifications and wants to reach out to you. It's freelance matchmaking at its finest.

Site 2: www.Elance.com

How it works: I see Elance.com as the closest competitor to Guru.com. As you do at Guru.com, you build a profile, search for and bid on projects, and get contacted by clients interested in your work. Payments are secure through the Elance network and you can show off a job well done through client feedback.

What I like: Elance does a nice job structuring the relationship between freelancer and client. You can set project milestone dates and even request payment at each milestone juncture.

Site 3: www.WritersMarket.com

How it works: Writer's Market is considered the Bible of freelance writing. You can check out the online site or buy the annual hard-copy book. Granted it's focused predominantly on freelance writing only, but if this is your revenue angle, then Writer's Market is worth a look.

What I like: Writer's Market makes it easy to search writing categories and find good leads for your expertise. You can even track manuscript submissions if you choose to advance from articles to full-length book writing.

Less Is More

The less work you have to do yourself, the more time you can free up for thinking big, acting big, or just plain enjoying your free time. Not only do I provide freelance services through Guru.com and Elance, but I also hire freelancers myself to build websites, complete research projects, design spreadsheets, or do anything else where my time is better spent elsewhere.

Site 4: www.GLGroup.com

How it works: Gerson Lehrman Group is a network of over 175,000 experts who get paid to complete client surveys and talk live with clients. How would you like to make $150 for filling out a simple survey? Or $200 for a one-hour phone call with a client interested in learning from your experience? Go to www.GLGroup.com, click on the "Councils" tab on the top left, and you're off and running.

What I like: I know there are people out there who could benefit from my expertise. But who has the time to find these people? GLGroup. com makes it easy by automatically matching my expertise with those willing to pay for it. Making $150 or $200 for an hour of work has never been easier.

Site 5: www.MomCorps.com

How it works: Don't cancel this site out just because you're a dad or you've never been married. Mom Corps is considered the expert in the field of flexible employment and caters to anyone who has opted out of the traditional corporate environment. Its goal is to help you continue working in your field of expertise while leaving plenty of time for family and nonwork-life needs.

What I like: The site posts flexible working opportunities in varied fields. Where else can you gain access to these unique job openings at some of the biggest names in business? The founders of the site also will contact you directly if they think you could be a good fit for a current opening.

Site 6: www.mediabistro.com

How it works: If you're a media professional, be sure to bookmark mediabistro.com. For opportunities in film, television, video, production, art/design, photography, publishing, advertising, and editorial, this is one-stop shopping for media mavens. Click on the Freelance Marketplace for access to a forum where you can showcase your work and get matched up with clients.

What I like: Mediabistro hosts cocktail parties and events for media professionals in major cities around the United States. These are fantastic networking opportunities for those who want to meet hundreds of industry professionals in one night.

Site 7: www.The-EFA.org

How it works: The Editorial Freelancers Association (EFA) is a national professional organization for writers, editors, proofreaders, desktop publishers, indexers, researchers, and translators. For a small annual fee, you'll gain access to job listings, peer networking, educational programs, and membership in a regional chapter of the association.

What I like: Are you worried about finding health-care benefits when you step off the corporate rat race? The EFA offers several health insurance plans at group rates including HMOs, long-term care insurance, and even dental insurance.

Ask Jeff_____

So how do you know which of the 10 sites to join? My recommendation is to join two or three, give it your all, and see how much business you drum up. It's more effective to deep-dive into a handful of sites than post generic profiles on all 10 just to get your name out. Over time you'll see which sites work best for you, and you can make adjustments from there.

Site 8: www.MyPartTimePro.com

How it works: Designed to meet the needs of part-time employees, this site is devoted to experienced professionals who simply no longer want a traditional corporate job. Opportunities include freelance gigs, virtual careers, job-share openings, seasonal employment, project-based work, and telecommuting. After posting your profile, you'll receive regular e-mails listing openings that match your skill set.

What I like: The service is free because costs are paid by employers who post openings. The site makes my job easy with the consistent e-mails highlighting jobs that meet the predetermined employment criteria I listed in my profile.

Site 9: www.GoFreelance.com

How it works: This site considers itself a freelance work exchange, designed to match freelancers and employers. Many of the opportunities are designed for folks who want to start legitimate home-based businesses. So if you've seen those "get rich quick" work-from-home opportunities and wondered where you could find the real gigs, this is your place.

What I like: It's nice to see that this site vets out the scams, leaving you with legitimate freelance opportunities. It can be hard to know from a website whether you can trust a particular gig, but at least with Go Freelance you know they've done their homework.

Site 10: www.iFreelance.com

How it works: With this site you can post your profile and immediately gain access to thousands of employers in need of your professional services. You can even advertise yourself to potential clients to score more business.

What I like: Many of the freelance sites take a commission when you land a gig. This is not the case with iFreelance.com, which means more money in your pocket when the work is done.

Freelance Strategy 3: Leveraging Industry Associations

Let's say you want to freelance in the world of human resources. Beyond power relationships and online sites, how else can you drive business to your front door? I've found industry associations to be an undervalued resource in landing more business.

People always ask me how you find the right association for you. Let's keep with the example of the human-resources professional. Go to Google and type in "human resources associations". In seconds you'll see four great human-resources associations to join:

- ◆ The National Human Resources Association (NHRA): www. HumanResoures.org

- ◆ Professionals in Human Resources Association (PIHRA): www. PIHRA.org

- ◆ Society for Human Resources Management (SHRM): www. SHRM.org

- ◆ The International Association for Human Resource Information Management (IHRIM): www.IHRIM.org

 Time and a Half

One of the quickest ways to build business fast is to connect with a mentor once you join an industry association. Go to your first meeting and see who impresses you. Introduce yourself and offer to take them to lunch. You can even offer your services to them for free in exchange for their advice. It's a barter arrangement well worth your time.

Joining a website alone is not what lands new business. Let's delve into one of the sites a bit deeper for all the resources available to members. If you look at www.SHRM.org, you'll notice members receive the following benefits:

♦ Membership Directory: Access to search names, titles, companies, and job functions of all the SHRM members

♦ HR Jobs Bulletin: Automatic e-mails when HR opportunities open up that meet your job-search criteria

♦ *HR Magazine:* Monthly magazine with the latest ideas, insights, and research in the world of human resources

♦ SHRM Surveys: Research on the latest trends and workplace issues facing human-resources professionals

♦ Seminars and Certificate Programs: Online and classroom training opportunities to enhance HR knowledge

♦ Local Chapters: A listing of nearly 600 SHRM local chapters for joining and networking

♦ Conferences: Worldwide listing of HR conferences, events, and expositions

Less Is More

You'll meet hundreds of people at an industry conference. That's great for networking but can be tough on making yourself memorable. The key is a tight elevator speech about you, your background, and services. If you can spout this out in 30 seconds or less, you'll make a better impression than fumbling through "Nice to meet you" and "Is this your first time here?"

That's just a partial list on the SHRM site. Can you imagine all the different ways you could build freelance HR business through these tools? What's that you say? You're not the imagining type? Okay, here are five concrete ways you could land freelance business from these resources:

♦ You could search the membership directory for new people to add to your network, reach out to them, and pitch new freelance business ideas.

♦ You could read the articles in *HR Magazine*, see the most current challenges facing HR professionals, and brainstorm ways you could solve these problems as a freelancer.

- You could buy a booth at an upcoming HR exposition and sell your freelance services to attendees.

- You could join the HR local chapter near your home and build a freelance client base.

- You could complete a certificate program to improve your HR skill set, add new HR freelance capabilities, and market these new skills to potential clients.

So this was just an example for the HR freelancer. Sub in your own freelance expertise and you get the idea. Industry associations are your ticket to more leads, more business, and most importantly bigger profits. Plus, by networking with people of similar interests and experience, you'll close sales faster. That will take care of the working less part of the equation.

How to Keep Your Freelance Pipeline Churning with Prospects

I'm about to save you from making the biggest freelance mistake imaginable! This is a mistake I made early on, and it cost me big time. Have I built up enough suspense yet? Are you dying to know the mistake and how to avoid it? Do you wish I'd stop asking questions and get on with it already? Okay, I hear your interest brewing. The biggest mistake newbie freelancers make is forgetting to consistently prospect for new business.

Notice I didn't say "prospect for new business." I said "*consistently* prospect for new business." When you start out with zero clients, of course you'll be fired up to land new business. Then you score a few new clients and you're flying high. You forget about prospecting and instead dive into pleasing your new clients with out-of-this-world effort. A few months go by, the checks start rolling in, you buy that flat-screen television you've been dreaming about, and life is good.

Then reality kicks in, the projects end, and you're back to square one. Now you're kicking yourself as the money train halts and the flat-screen television gets repossessed. If you want the train to keep making stops and the television to stay mounted on your wall, you'll want to follow a game plan to keep your freelance pipeline churning with prospects.

Ask Jeff _____

What if you really don't have the time to prospect for new business? Or what if you just don't like fishing for clients? There are companies out there, like www. SalesGenie.com, that will provide fresh new leads for a fee. Consider this strategy like outsourcing your sales efforts to free up your time for growing other sides of your freelance business.

Having learned this lesson the hard way, I'm going to save you time and aggravation by breaking down exactly what I do now to keep a steady stream of new and repeat clients. The key to making these steps work for you is to realize one simple fact about prospecting for business:

There should be zero connection between the number of clients you have and the time you spend prospecting for business. Whether you're juggling 20 clients or 1, you need to keep the same focus on ensuring your future is filled with new business rolling in.

With this simple prospecting fact in mind, here is your five-step game plan:

1. **Cherish your current clients.** Let's say you were a mint chocolate chip ice cream salesman. Who would be an easier sell, someone who never bought from you before or someone who downed a deluxe cone last week? Repeat business is so much easier than new business.

   When I land a client, I treat that client like gold. First, I over-deliver on my work to ensure satisfaction. Second, I check in with the client regularly to see what else is keeping her up at night. Her answers are the key to repeat business.

2. **Contact your Rolodex regularly.** Four times per year I send something to my network of 1,000 people. It could be a simple holiday card or an e-mail about my latest projects and freelance offerings.

   Over time, I've seen that four is a good number. You're in touch enough to never be forgotten but not so much that you're viewed as a pest. Every time I mass contact, a few folks respond back with preliminary interest.

3. **Work the Rolodex nibbles.** Contacting 1,000 people four times per year can seem like a lot of work. But the real work kicks in when you get responses. You've got to be ready to act and follow up on those nibbles.

When someone writes back, I check my files to refresh my memory of his background, job title, and responsibilities. That quick check gives me the ammunition to respond back and move the conversation forward toward potential freelance business.

 Fear Busters _____

Some freelancers are afraid of their own success. They actually fear too many people chomping at the bit to benefit from their services. Remember, a manager can never have too many good pitchers, and a freelancer can never have too many new clients. You never know when a trusted client will walk out the door, making you awfully glad you have the new leads rolling in.

4. **Stay active online and at industry associations.** You should definitely congratulate yourself if you've taken the time to sign up for a bunch of online freelance sites and industry associations. That's a great first step in building out your network.

However, joining is only the beginning. People make this mistake all the time with health clubs. They think joining is all it takes to lose weight, tone those muscles, and improve stamina. But you've got to go to the gym regularly to see those results. Networking online and through industry associations is the same. Joining is step one, but the payoff comes from regular and consistent interaction.

5. **Strive for client predictability.** Open-ended assignments are a freelancer's worst nightmare. You have no idea how long a project will go or how much money you'll make. That can make it awfully tough to figure out how much new business you need to land at any one time.

I strive for client predictability by jointly agreeing on project timelines, payments, and major milestones. This way, I know if I'm locked up for two weeks or two months. It also gives me an opportunity to renegotiate if a freelance gig starts falling outside the original parameters.

There you have it ... five steps to make sure your first clients aren't your last. Follow these steps and your freelance career will lead to working less and earning more than you ever thought possible. Ignore the advice and it's a surefire path to working more and earning less.

The Least You Need to Know

- Unlike starving artists, freelancers can earn significant income through their passions.

- Knowing the right people can exponentially grow the number of new projects coming your way.

- Sites abound on the Internet where you can post your experience and get matched up with clients needing your services.

- There's an industry association for just about every skill, expertise, and passion; be sure to join the one that suits you.

- Continuously prospecting for new business is the best way to keep a steady flow of new clients on the horizon.

7

Running a Business Without Ruining Your Life

In This Chapter

◆ Running a profitable business without running yourself into the ground

◆ Learning to delegate as a means to duplicate your efforts on a grander scale

◆ Following the scent of money and putting more energy into your most profitable business ideas

◆ Taking on partners or getting out of a business that has you in over your head

So you own the cutest little flower shop your town ever did see. Or you run the quickest copy and print shop this side of the Mississippi. Or a great idea hit you over drinks and the business plan is sketched on a cocktail napkin. Whatever your business idea or stage of development, this is the chapter for you, the business owner.

Now I know most business owners are quite emotional about their little babies. The business gets more love, time, and attention than everything else except the spouse and kids. In some cases, the spouse and kids might actually feel they run a distant second to the business. I'm here to tell you small businesses are not allergic to earning more and working less. In fact, just like consulting, freelancing, and Internet marketing, you can watch your wallet fatten while your free time blossoms.

In this chapter, I start by breaking the mindset that a successful business requires every waking hour. Next, you can look at what it takes to run a business and which of those tasks should be outsourced or left to your employees. You can then look at the different ways your business makes money and see if you can shift some energy to your most profitable opportunities. Finally, you take a hard look at your business to see if another partner or maybe selling out and starting over is in your best interests. So Mr. or Ms. Small Business Owner, are you ready to "own" up to what it takes to earn more and work less while running a business?

Breaking the Mentality That Your Business Is Your Life

The moment I left corporate America, I felt a sense of relief. I was no longer a small cog in a big machine. I was now my own man, capable of making my own rules and charting my own path. After a few days of chest-pounding, my pride turned to fear as I realized being your own man means making your own money. It turns out I had grown quite accustomed to that friendly direct-deposit paycheck every two weeks.

A fear of bouncing checks, declaring bankruptcy, and proving all the naysayers right was enough to motivate me. I did what anyone would do ... dove into making money. The problem with this approach is it puts the spotlight on earning more while eliminating the second most important goal, working less. This mistaken belief that your business is your life can sabotage the very reason you left your other gig in the first place. Still, breaking this mindset can be hard to do. Lucky for you, I'm just the guy who can make that mindset break for you.

Without further ado, here are the top 10 reasons business owners turn their businesses into their life and what you can do about it.

Reason 1: You Don't Trust Anyone with Your Little Baby

The brilliant idea for a gourmet chocolate bar with organic walnuts hit you in the middle of a train ride from Boston to New York. Your start-up enthusiasm led to countless hours in the kitchen perfecting the recipe. Even your mom now admits this is the best-tasting chocolate bar she's ever eaten.

Going from a delicious kitchen prototype to a best-selling marketplace product is going to require more than just you. But as you meet manufacturers, retailers, and packagers you feel an overwhelming desire to take on these tasks yourself. These new partners simply don't show the passion for your product. How can you trust them to put enough energy into helping your idea succeed?

You've got to remind yourself that even though others will influence your product's success, you still have the most skin in the game. You gave up the corporate job to become Ms. Chocolate. You invested part of your retirement fund in start-up costs. So of course you're going to show the most outward emotions. But taking on the entire production process is a mistake, mainly because you're failing to rely on the expertise of others. Sure you created the recipe, but can you really claim to know the ins and outs of chocolate retailing? Find the right partners, give them a shot to do what they do best, and you'll be more successful without burning the midnight chocolate oil.

Reason 2: You Believe There's a Direct Correlation Between Hours Worked and Income Earned

You run a dry-cleaning business and believe staying open 24 hours is the surest way to corner the market. Anytime a guy needs a shirt pressed at 3:30 A.M. or a businesswoman needs a blouse ironed at 5 A.M., you'll be the surefire dry cleaner of choice.

A funny thing happens as you patiently wait for customers from midnight until sunrise. Nobody comes in. Despite the fact that you're the

Time and a Half

If you're just starting up your new business, you can learn tons of useful information in no time through the Small Business Administration (SBA). Established by the United States Government to aid start-ups, you can gain instant access to training, financial advice, and a network of small business offices in every state. Check out www.sba.gov to learn more.

only dry cleaner opened, customers seem content to sleep through the night and tackle their wrinkled clothes the next day.

Nobody can argue there's a correlation between effort exerted and resulting payoff. Certainly staying open late two nights per week can bring in business from folks who work late themselves. But at some point the payoff from extra hours levels off. You've got to recognize that point of diminishing returns, change that part of your business strategy, and eliminate the unnecessary hours.

Reason 3: You Fear Your Competitors Will Put You Out of Business

You run a local taxi service and employ 20 drivers. Two other competitors have set up shop in town, and the three companies battle it out daily for cab fare. You begin to see your competitors as the enemy and assume they're spending every waking hour trying to crush you. Not to be outworked, you wake up early and go to bed late developing counter-strategies to put them out of business first.

Are your competitors really the biggest obstacle to your success? Does your focus need to be on them, or could you benefit more from improving your own taxi service? Sometimes it's easy to get so caught up in crushing the competition you forget what makes a business successful. It's more than just making your competitors look bad; you've got to offer an enticing product or service yourself. Instead of going to war with your competitors, some simple enhancements to your taxi service offerings might catapult your business to the next level.

Reason 4: You Worked All Hours of the Night to Get Your Business off the Ground

Starting a boutique cell-phone store took blood, sweat, tears, and just about every weekend for the last two years. Now that you're up and running, the last thing you want to do is slow down and lose momentum. So you keep the same hours, work seven days a week, and make sure your early efforts continue as the business grows.

Is it possible that the level of effort to get off the ground is not equal to the effort required to run the business? Maybe, just maybe, you're working these long hours because it's become your weekly routine. You're accustomed to ordering Chinese takeout every Thursday at 9 P.M. and you actually like chatting up the package delivery guy on Saturday mornings. What started as a strong work ethic has now become a hard habit to break.

Remember, just because you're used to working 100 hours per week doesn't mean you have to do it for eternity. It's time to check in on what you're doing during all these hours to see if you really need the full 100 anymore.

Reason 5: You Believe Taking on a Bigger Staff Will Bleed Your Income Dry

You own a popular Italian restaurant in a trendy part of the city. As fate would have it, the shoe store next door went belly up. The opportunity presents itself to knock down the wall and expand your restaurant. Within three months you could go from 20 to 30 tables.

The income potential excites you, but the thought of hiring more staff scares you beyond belief. What if you add the 10 extra tables, but the additional customers don't show? That's when the idea hits you to take on more responsibility yourself rather than ramp up staff. You waited tables in college; certainly it will come back to you easily.

The fear of paying more staff for new business yet to materialize is a fair concern. But it shouldn't swing you all the way to doubling your own hours. Perhaps you can do some market research first to see if the bigger restaurant is likely to succeed. Or you can hire the additional staff slowly as new customers materialize.

Reason 6: You're Hiding from Something in Your Personal Life You'd Rather Not Face

Your car dealership is a hit. The cars sell faster than you can keep them on the lot. Your dealership is so successful it practically runs on autopilot. Still, you choose to work 60 hours per week despite the fact you could easily get by with 30.

Why all the extra hours? It turns out the relationship with your spouse is in trouble. Rather than face another night of fighting, you bury yourself in paperwork at the office. You figure some relationship distance could do you and your spouse good.

The problem with hiding at the office is that problems in your personal life rarely get better on their own. Avoiding, delaying, and procrastinating serve only to put personal problems on hold. You just may find that facing your problems head on will both move you toward resolution and enable you to work the 30, not 60, hours required to get the job done.

Reason 7: You Need a Refresher Course in Time Management

It's 11 A.M. and you peek your head out to check the customer flow at your bakery. You've been at work since 5:30 A.M. making sure to catch the morning commuters looking for muffins and bagels. Business is good as the customers shuffle in and out to enjoy their morning treats.

Suddenly it hits you. While you've been at work for five and a half hours, your only accomplishments are checking e-mails, buttering a few bagels during the busy period, and calling one supplier to negotiate a new price for baking good ingredients. Where did your time go?

Days have a way of slipping away if you don't take control. Maybe simple to-do lists or daily/weekly goals will make the difference in getting more done in less time. At the very least you won't feel that failed sense of getting nothing done throughout the day.

Less Is More _____

When you make a to-do list at the beginning of the day, the more unnecessary tasks listed, the less important stuff gets done. If you absolutely must list everything you want to get done that day, at least kick off your work with the absolute most important task.

Reason 8: You Spend Too Much Time on What You Enjoy Most About Your Business

You run a flower shop downtown. From weddings to special events, you're one of the biggest providers of floral arrangements in the entire city. The local paper just ran a profile of your business, and customers are now flocking to your store.

Above everything else, your absolute favorite activity is personally arranging the flowers. You have an eye for it and can't help spending countless hours getting the flowers to sit just right. If you could put 100 percent of your energy into flower arranging, you'd do it in a heartbeat.

The question is whether the floral arrangements bring in the big bucks. Is it your signature layout that keeps the customers rolling in? Or is it really about price, location, or speed of delivery? Countless hours on what you enjoy most works well for passions, but it's not a great strategy for working less in a small business. Take the time to see if your passion is aligned with the true moneymakers in your business model.

Reason 9: You're Underutilizing Technology to Speed Up Processes and Improve Procedures

You built your bookkeeping business with pen and paper. You've got 30 loyal customers who depend on you to balance their books. Your manual processes may take longer, but you really dig the Mom-and-Pop feel of your business.

Over the years technology advances have led to the introduction of automated bookkeeping spreadsheets. Projects that used to take hours can now be done literally in minutes. Still, you stick with old-fashioned pen and paper. You have your systems, and you're comfortable, so why change?

Here's a good reason to change … you're staying up way past your bedtime with pen and paper when technology could have you in bed by 9 P.M. Your customers care more about the accuracy of your work than the means of getting the work done. It can be tough to change with the times, but if you truly want to work less you've got to pay attention to technology upgrades.

Reason 10: You Believe Your Customers Will Notice Your Extra Effort

Five years ago you left your big-city law firm to start up a small-town solo gig. You've developed a reputation for winning big bucks for plaintiffs in civil litigation lawsuits. You pride yourself on answering the phone at all hours of the night and taking appointments on a moment's notice.

Sure, customers appreciate your availability, but is this really the reason you continue to win new business? Are new plaintiffs calling you because they know you'll answer the phone at 10 P.M. or because their friend referred them to you?

Late-night and short-notice availability is only worth it if it truly differentiates you from the competition. Perhaps some informal customer feedback could tell you if in fact the all-hour availability is a customer pleaser or an unnecessary offering.

Learning the Power of Delegation and Outsourcing

It's time for another one-question quiz. I'm awarding extra points for honesty on this one. Here we go:

You own a large book shop in a suburban strip mall. The trash right under the main cash register is heavy and full. Do you …

> Choice A: Ask your cashier to take the trash out and get back to running your business?
>
> Choice B: Ask your cashier to take the trash out and then check back in an hour to see if the task is complete?
>
> Choice C: Inform your cashier the trash is full and then walk with him to the curb to jointly take out the trash?
>
> Choice D: Wait until your cashier goes on break and then take the trash out yourself?

Choice E: Hire a trash collection service to empty the waste baskets around the store so that neither you nor the cashier need to do it?

What does trash have to do with delegation and outsourcing? More on that in a moment. Right now I'm curious which choice you selected. Don't choose what you believe is the right way to handle the situation. Choose the option that best describes how you would likely handle the situation. Did you lock in your answer? Great, now let's break it down:

> **Fear Busters**
>
> Too many small business owners are afraid to be honest about their situation. If you're a control freak, micro-manager, or overly critical boss, let's call it out already. Your management style just might be the biggest obstacle to working less and earning more. Start trusting others with tasks that don't make or break your business. You'll be glad you did.

♦ If you picked Choice A, then you already practice best-in-class delegation. You also likely hired a great cashier, someone you can count on to get a task done without additional follow-ups.

♦ If you picked Choice B, delegation is your strong suit but you've got to question why you need to check up on your employee. Are you taking an unnecessary extra step, or does your cashier's prior performance warrant the double check?

♦ If you picked Choice C, then I just might need to call you a "control freak" in the best sense of the word. Either you're doubling the resources on a task easily accomplished by one person or you're way too concerned with trash disposal to let your cashier handle the task alone.

♦ If you picked Choice D, you're choosing to do a task better left for cheaper labor. As the owner of the small business, your time should be viewed as the most valuable. The more time invested in simple tasks, the less time left for more important to-do items like generating new business.

♦ If you picked Choice E, you've advanced beyond delegation to the world of outsourcing. You've discovered that some tasks can be done for even cheaper than the price of labor in your store. By outsourcing these tasks, you can raise the game of cashiers and have them focus on reconciling receipts, calling customers, or restacking the shelves.

Here's the bottom line from this one-question quiz and this section of the book: if you truly want to work less and earn more, you'll need to get awfully comfortable with delegating and outsourcing tasks that either take too long or don't generate revenue.

I'm sure you're thinking right now that delegating means hiring a staff and outsourcing means hiring contractors. Both ideas cost money and can easily wipe out the earning-more part of the equation. I absolutely agree with you. The idea is not to delegate and outsource just for the sake of clearing your to-do list. The goal is to figure out what your time is worth and then hand off those tasks that fall outside your time and money calculations.

Did I just lose you? No problem, let's break down an example to bring this concept to life. Pretend the following is true of your small business:

- ◆ You own an exclusive hair salon on a small side street in your local town.

- ◆ Your salon generates $200,000 in revenue each year.

- ◆ You personally work five days per week, 50 weeks per year, for a total of 2,000 hours per year.

 Time and a Half

Are you thinking of giving up your corporate gig to start a hair salon or other small business? Hit the ground running by checking out the Service Corps of Retired Executives (www.score.org). Boasting a team of more than 10,000 former executives, the Corps provides you free face-to-face and e-mail support in launching your little baby.

So what's your time worth? Well, you can divide your annual revenue by the hours worked to determine what you're earning for every hour you devote to the salon.

$200,000 ÷ 2,000 hours = $100 per hour

Earning $100 for every hour worked is nothing to sneeze at. Most folks would call that a pretty nice living. But maybe, just maybe, a closer look at delegation and outsourcing could swing the equation even further in your favor. To get our answer, we first need to brainstorm a list of all the activities associated with running your hair salon. Here's just a partial list I developed from looking around the salon the last time I shortened my bangs:

♦ Sweeping the floor throughout the day as hair gets clipped from the heads of customers

♦ Answering the phone during business hours to take new appointments and change existing appointments

♦ Balancing the books to make sure customers are paying, credit card bills reconcile, and cash flow looks good

♦ Hiring and managing a staff of hair stylists to serve the flow of customers

♦ Purchasing and maintaining scissors, brushes, shampoos, and clippers for use by your staff

♦ Advertising in local newspapers, radio, or television to spread the word about your business and attract new customers

♦ Choosing a line of hair-care products to sell at checkout as an add-on revenue generator for your business

♦ Dealing with contractors and vendors, such as landlords, utility companies, and plumbers, on a regular basis

♦ Cleaning the restroom at your salon every night to keep it fresh and clean for your customers

♦ Hanging decorations as various holidays approach to show your spirit and support the community

♦ Preparing your taxes every April and submitting proper documentation to the Internal Revenue Service

♦ Building and maintaining your company website to create an online presence for your business

♦ Shoveling snow out front when storms hit and regularly washing the entranceway to clear debris from your storefront

◆ Servicing your salon chairs regularly to keep them functioning properly, ensuring comfort for your customers

◆ Managing payroll, tips, and bonuses for your staff to get everyone paid fairly and on time

Okay, let's get down to business. Assume for a moment that the owner of this salon currently manages all 15 tasks alone. That's right, from shoveling snow to hanging decorations and managing the staff, this entrepreneur is a real go-getter. The question becomes, how can we apply earning more and working less to this hair salon? Could we find a way to raise her income while cutting her hours? Let's draw a line in the sand and see whether we can raise her revenue to $250,000 while cutting her hours from 2,000 per year to 1,900. That extra hundred hours of free time equals two and a half more weeks of vacation. Not sure about you, but I'll gladly sign up for an extra $50,000 in revenue plus four and a half weeks of total vacation each year. Not a bad life if you ask me. But how do we really make this a reality? Let's roll up our sleeves and crunch some numbers while looking at both delegation and outsourcing opportunities.

First, what could the hair salon owner delegate to her staff to free up her own time? Right away I see three good candidates:

> **Less Is More**
>
> Why do so many small-business owners take on running their businesses alone? Maybe it's a you-against-the-world mentality or lack of trust in anyone but yourself. The reality is the more you can outsource and delegate menial tasks, the more time you'll have left over to think big and grow your business.

◆ *Decoration hanging:* You give one of your hair stylists the afternoon off once per month to buy and hang decorations. This costs you $5,000 annually in lost haircutting time.

◆ *Appointment calls:* You bring in a receptionist to make and change appointments for $25,000 per year.

◆ *Salon sweeping:* You set up a rotating calendar of sweeping responsibilities for all your stylists. This costs you $5,000 annually in lost haircutting time.

Okay, now how about outsourcing? Which of the 15 tasks could be outsourced for a fee? Again, I see three good candidates without looking too hard:

♦ *Tax preparation:* For $1,500 per year, you can find a suitable tax professional to gather the paperwork and submit it to the IRS.

♦ *Payroll services:* Companies like ADP can handle all your payroll needs for a small fee; let's assume $6,000 per year.

♦ *Restroom cleanup:* You arrange for a cleaning service to stop by at end of day and tidy up for $7,500 annually.

Let's see where we stand. We've delegated and outsourced 6 of the 15 activities. The total cost of these six activities adds up to $50,000. Right now four facts are true about the hair salon business:

Fact 1: Delegation and outsourcing of these six activities has freed up 200 hours of the owner's time.

Fact 2: Revenue is temporarily down from $200,000 to $150,000.

Fact 3: Our goal is to raise revenue to $250,000, so we need to find $100,000 in new business to hit our target.

Fact 4: Our goal is to hit 1,900 in annual hours for the owner, so we have an extra 100 hours to use.

You can probably guess how this owner should use this newfound 100 hours—finding a way to make an extra $100,000 annually. A funny thing happens when an owner takes her mind off the daily minutiae of running the business. Suddenly new ideas seep through, the kind of ideas that can lead to big bucks. Our newly freed-up owner takes advantage of the extra 100 hours and implements three new business ideas:

♦ A previously unused corner of the salon offers manicures for waiting customers. The manicurist costs $20,000 per year, but she generates $60,000 in new revenue. That's an extra $40,000 in our owner's pocket.

♦ The owner analyzes the sales figures for the various hair-care products on sale at checkout. She swaps out underselling items for new, higher-end products and sees an immediate boost in sales. In fact, the simple move of product swapping generates $50,000 annually in additional sales.

◆ The landlord comes by to renew the lease. Instead of quickly signing to get back to work, the owner takes some time to negotiate.
She convinces the landlord to offer a $10,000 annual discount if
she signs a longer-term lease.

You guessed it; we've hit our $100,000 additional revenue target by
investing the newfound 100 hours wisely. Our hair salon owner can
now officially join the working-less, earning-more club. She's raised
annual revenues from $200,000 to $250,000 while cutting her annual
hours from 2,000 to 1,900. I know you can do the same if you take a
close look at delegation and outsourcing in your business.

Shifting Personal Energy to the Cash Cows

Let's cut ties (pun intended) with our hair salon business as we begin
our cash-cow discussion. In a nutshell, this section is all about finding
the true money-makers, also known as cash cows, in your business and
shifting your energy to squeeze as much profit in as little time out of
those cash cows. For the purpose of this section, let's assume you own
a coffee shop in the center of town. At first glance, we learn a few facts
about your coffee shop:

Fact 1: Similar to the hair salon, the coffee shop generates
$200,000 in revenue each year.

Fact 2: As the owner, you also are spending 2,000 hours per year
running your business.

Fact 3: Your coffee shop is about more than just great-tasting coffee. You also sell grab-and-go breakfast and lunch items, coffee
accessories such as mugs and coffee makers, as well as homemade
coffee beans.

Ask Jeff _____

What if you can't run the numbers on your own coffee shop because
your start-up is still in the idea phase? A great first step is to create a
business plan; Bplans.com can help sketch your business out in no time.
With sample plans, a template to fill out, and expert online guidance,
you'll put pen to paper (or should I say finger to keyboard) in no time.

Fact 4: Beyond selling coffee and related products, you also make money selling CDs played in the coffee shop as well as unique gift books and games.

To discover your cash cow, we need to look at how you earn your $200,000. Specifically we need to examine how much time and money it takes to generate each of your revenue channels. A closer look at your business reveals the following information.

Product	Revenue Generated	Cost to Offer Product
Coffee	$30,000	$7,000
Tea	$10,000	$5,000
Breakfast	$35,000	$9,000
Lunch	$5,000	$6,000
Coffee mugs	$2,500	$1,000
Coffee makers	$2,500	$3,000
Coffee beans	$50,000	$25,000
Music CDs	$50,000	$15,000
Gift books	$10,000	$4,000
Games	$5,000	$3,000
TOTAL	$200,000	$78,000

To keep things simple, let's assume you divide your 2,000 annual hours evenly among these 10 revenue channels. So you spend 200 hours per year marketing and selling each of your 10 products. What are some of the stories that emerge from this table?

♦ Two products, coffee beans and music CDs, generate 50 percent ($100,000) of your annual revenue ($200,000) while costing you slightly more than 50 percent ($40,000) of your total costs ($78,000).

♦ Two products, lunch and coffee makers, cost you more to offer ($9,000) than the revenue they generate ($7,500).

♦ Two products, coffee and breakfast, generate the highest margins at around three times their cost.

♦ Two products, coffee mugs and coffee makers, generate just $5,000 of your $200,0000 in revenue while still costing you 20 percent (400) of the 2,000 hours you work each year.

Fear Busters

Do words like "revenue" and "margin" confuse you more than a one-way sign on a dead-end street? Have no fear; check out the National Society of Accountants (www. nsacct.org) for some expert advice. From accounting support to management advisory services, you'll benefit from this 17,000+ member organization.

This is the fun part. Now we get to slice and dice this data until we find the perfect combination of earning more and working less. We're looking for which of the 10 products generate the most revenue at the best margin with the least amount of time spent possible. Similar to the hair salon, let's look for cash cows for the purpose of raising our revenue to $250,000 while working just 1,900 hours.

How can we meet our goal? After crunching some numbers, we might realize the following four steps will make it happen:

1. **Stop serving lunch and selling coffee makers.** Every lunch you serve and every coffee maker you sell actually loses money for you. Right away you can get back 400 annual hours of your time by eliminating these two offerings.

2. **Fill the old coffeemaker shelf space with coffee beans and music CDs.** Now that the bulky coffee makers are history, fill that open shelf space with two of your best-selling products, coffee beans and music CDs.

3. **Expand your coffee and breakfast offerings.** Your best margins come from coffee and breakfast. You could start offering more coffee flavors and adding an hour on the front and back end of your breakfast hours. If you are cutting lunch hours, this does not even add to your workload. You might even introduce some new breakfast treats like muffins and bagels.

4. **Swap out the coffee mugs and gift books with more expensive designer products.** The mugs and gift books deliver pretty solid margins. Maybe you could improve those margins even further by selling higher-end products. You could charge more while keeping shelf space the same.

Put these four moves together and you just might find even more than an extra $50,000 in annual revenue while still reducing your hours spent on the job. At the very least, you'll be focusing your efforts on the cash cows, those products that generate the best margins and revenues for the least effort.

Hard Decisions: Taking on Partners and/or Selling Out

We know you're a go-getter. We realize you possess that unique entrepreneurial spirit. We congratulate you for risking it all to make your dream business a reality. Unfortunately, accolades alone are not enough to make your business successful. Or the business may be generating a solid income, but it's not in line with your working-less, earning-more goals. Sometimes your best move can be asking for a helping hand or getting out of the business entirely and starting something new.

But how do you make these difficult decisions? This section is all about arriving at the all-important decision of taking on partners or selling out and starting over. Let's take these one at a time because taking on partners represents growing your business through another pair of helping hands. Selling or dissolving your business is a completely different direction where you make a clean break and start fresh.

Should You Bring a Partner on Board?

Asking for help can be an emotional decision. It can feel like a sign of failure. You couldn't go it alone, so you're raising the white flag and admitting you don't have what it takes to run a solo gig.

I prefer to view partners as a potential blessing. The right new blood just might be the perfect jump-start to catapult your business into the land of earning more and working less. But before you open your doors to another pair of hands, be sure to ask yourself the following five questions:

◆ Question 1: Will a new partner share your vision for the business?

The only thing worse than struggling alone is bringing on a partner paddling in a different direction. You'll want to make sure a partner shares your business goals, otherwise you'll be at odds from the get-go.

Ask Jeff

How do you cut a good deal when you take on a partner? It likely comes down to the art of effective negotiating. If you're a novice when it comes to deal-making, you'll want to visit the Negotiation Resource Center at www.Batna.com. Created by Eric C. Gould, the site is full of negotiation tips, advice, resources, and training materials.

♦ Question 2: Will a new partner contribute to your working-less, earning-more agenda?

Maybe a new partner will double your revenue while cutting your personal time working by 30 percent. Or maybe just the opposite will happen, revenue will drop and you'll be working twice as hard. Get on the same page with your revenue and working goals from the outset.

♦ Question 3: Does your partner bring something new to the table?

There's no reason to partner with your virtual twin. The idea is to add to the overall skill set of your business. If you're an expert salesperson, maybe you need a number cruncher to take your business to the next level.

♦ Question 4: What's your relationship with the potential partner?

There's a big difference between bringing your brother on board and putting an ad in the local paper. Both approaches come with their pros and cons, so understand the trust and compatibility issues as you consider each direction or someone right in between.

♦ Question 5: Would an employee be more valuable than a partner?

Do you really need another pair of hands with an equal stake in the business? Maybe what your company really needs is a worker bee who can crank out the busywork while you strategically grow the business.

Should You Sell or Dissolve Your Business?

If you thought asking for help was difficult, you can only imagine how much more difficult it is to say good-bye to your baby. Now you're actually taking that big step and admitting that no amount of help, new products, or new services can salvage your idea. But you've also got to look on the bright side. You'll have learned a ton in the process and can apply those learnings to your next big idea.

> **Time and a Half**
>
> Are you looking for a quick way to find out what your business is really worth? Wondering if you could sell your business for big bucks? Check out Business Valuation Research, Inc. (www.business-value.com) for an objective and unbiased appraisal of your business. It just might help you set the market as you seek buyout prospects.

Admitting all of your hours didn't add up to a successful venture is no easy moment. Just remember, many of the most successful entrepreneurs failed over and over again before hitting it big with the right idea. Sometimes saying good-bye to the wrong idea represents just the right move to clear your mind for the million-dollar idea. If you're heading toward selling or dissolving your business, be sure to ask these five questions to make a good decision:

♦ Question 1: Have you exhausted every angle to succeed?

Is it the idea that's failing or your approach to the business? Maybe a fresh look, a new approach, or some outside expertise could salvage your efforts before you sell or close up shop.

♦ Question 2: Do you have another idea ready to go?

If you're chomping at the bit to start something else, maybe your current business is actually holding you back. Just be sure there's something planned to fall back on, even if it's a short project stint with a former employer or client to tide you over.

♦ Question 3: Could selling provide the seed money for something better?

Maybe your first idea is moderately successful, but it's your next idea that will really hit the jackpot. Selling now could produce the perfect combination of investment dollars and some much-needed time off to make your next idea a reality.

♦ Question 4: Could a new partner or more employees save the day?

Fear Busters

Does your failed business venture have you on the verge of personal bankruptcy? Before your financial situation spirals out of control, visit ABI World (www.abiworld.org) for some much-needed help. Sponsored by the American Bankruptcy Institute, ABI World provides everything from information on bankruptcy legislation to help finding a bankruptcy professional. It's a great place to start when you feel the financial walls caving in.

Perhaps your idea is solid; you just don't have enough man power to make it successful. It could be that you're mistakenly considering selling or dissolving the business when taking on a partner or hiring more staff could be your ticket to success.

◆ Question 5: Do you have what it takes to run a business?

Working less and earning more could be the right lifestyle for you, but maybe running a small business doesn't match your personality. Would freelancing, consulting, or Internet marketing be a better source of income?

It might even be worth surfing around www.Entrepreneur.com, chock-full of information for small business owners, to see if you fit the bill.

The Least You Need to Know

◆ You can run a profitable business without devoting every waking hour to your little baby.

◆ You'll never get it all done if you don't master the power of delegating.

◆ Putting equal energy into all business aspects prevents you from maximizing income available from your cash cows.

◆ Sometimes taking on partners or selling a business off is the best move you can make to earn more and work less.

"Get Rich Slow" Passive Income Techniques

In This Chapter

- Why passive income is the secret to doubling and tripling your profits without exerting extra energy

- How to successfully invest in real estate when your last name is not Trump

- How to sell online products, services, and information to a loyal cyber customer base

- Techniques for earning royalties for life even if you don't have a hit single or sitcom in you

- Ways to make new business friends and make more money together through joint ventures

You're sitting in your pajamas polishing off the remnants of a vanilla fudge swirl pint of frozen yogurt. The clock strikes midnight as you mindlessly flip through the channels. It's infomercial hour, and the get-rich-quick schemes are coming fast and furious:

- ♦ Make millions in real estate with nothing down
- ♦ Earn $10,000 per week from home without selling a thing
- ♦ Call this 800-number in the next three minutes and you can instantly turn your debt into a dream house

Normally you'd laugh at these preposterous promises, but you're coming off a long week at work. Maybe, just maybe, one of these get-rich-quick schemes is legit. You dial the number, plunk down your hard-earned dollars, and watch the sales promise fizzle quicker than an Alka-Seltzer.

We've all been there. Tough weeks at work make you believe there has to be a better way. Those smiling and reassuring infomercial salespeople can be pretty convincing. But this chapter is going to take the opposite approach. Instead of selling you a bag of fool's gold, I'm going to teach you real ways to slowly but surely build passive income.

From real estate investing to online products and services to earning royalties, you're about to get the inside scoop on passive income strategies that really work. So turn off the late-night television, back away from the frozen yogurt, and let's make some money together.

The Difference Between Active and Passive Income

Here's a simple question ... which scenario sounds better?

- ♦ You work for your money
- ♦ Your money works for you

In the first scenario, money is your boss and you are the employee. In the second scenario, you're the boss and money works for you. Unless you have some deep-rooted desire to report directly to money, I'd recommend choosing the second scenario.

This is the basic difference between active and passive income. Active income requires your presence because you only get paid when you're working. Passive income comes your way when you're sleeping, eating, or chilling with friends. In my old corporate America life, just about everyone I knew earned 100 percent of their revenue through active income. Now that I'm working less and earning more, I've met hundreds of new friends who earn 50 percent or more of their profits through passive income.

Let's bring the difference to life through some examples of each kind of income. Active income would include ...

- A plumber who gets paid $79 per hour when on the job unclogging sinks, installing new pipes, and fixing water heaters.

- A marketing executive who earns $150,000 per year working in a Fortune 500 company.

- A human resources consultant who charges $1,500 per day to help organizations improve their leadership capabilities.

- A dermatologist who charges patients set fees for mole screenings, acne treatment, and Botox injections.

- A lawyer who charges $300 per hour to defend clients against civil lawsuits.

- A public speaker who gets paid $2,500 every time she delivers a keynote address in front of an audience.

What do the plumber, marketing executive, HR consultant, dermatologist, lawyer, and public speaker have in common? They all have to be physically working to earn their hourly, daily, flat-fee, and annual income. In all six examples, 100 percent of their income is earned through active means.

Does that mean these six professions are doomed to a life of solely active income? Not at all. Let's take the same six examples and show how each person could supplement their active income with a passive income channel:

- The plumber can sell containers of unclogging formulas and offer to mail refills every three months to keep drains running smoothly.

- The marketing executive can earn stock options or restricted stock awards that appreciate in value as long as he stays with the same company.

- The human resources consultant can develop an online leadership training module and license it to clients as an add-on product in conjunction with consulting engagements.

- The dermatologist can develop an acne treatment kit for patients to apply regularly at home for complexion improvement.

- The lawyer can write a book about beating civil lawsuits based on his experience and sell it at local bookstores.

- The public speaker can record one of her presentations and start selling it through the Internet.

Ask Jeff

What if you're struggling to come up with a passive income idea associated with your job? First, think if there's any product you could package together with your job that clients might want. Second, do you possess any unique information that a wider audience might pay to learn through a book or tape? Finally, could anything you do be repackaged in an online format to sell on the Internet?

In essence, any profession and any active income channel has the potential to generate supplemental passive income as well. I make this point because I don't want you to mistakenly believe quitting your job is a prerequisite for earning passive income. You absolutely can discover a passive channel in your job, earning that extra money for working the same hours or even cutting back your hours once the passive income starts rolling in.

As you know by now, my working-less and earning-more lifestyle consists of both active and passive income strategies. On the active front, I make money from human resources consulting gigs; writing books, articles, and blogs; delivering seminars; and completing free-lance projects. However, because I only want to work three to four days maximum per week, I've learned to supplement this active income with passive strategies that simply don't require my presence. Examples of a few of my top channels include:

- Owning a two-family rental property that generates positive cash flow even after the mortgage, taxes, and interest are paid as well as the landscaping fees, water bill, and wear and tear.

- Selling e-books, CDs, and tele-seminars through various channels online.

- Earning biannual royalty checks for the books I've written based on sales figures.

There you have it. This is a sample of the active and passive income combination that enables me to work less and earn more. I make my biggest active dollars from consulting (which we covered in Chapter 5) and freelance writing (which we covered in Chapter 6). Now it's time to get into my top three passive strategies:

1. Real estate investing

2. Online products and services

3. Royalty payments from books

 Fear Busters _____

I know what you're thinking ... how could consulting plus freelance plus real estate plus online products plus royalties possibly take less work than a standard 9-to-5 job? First off, most standard jobs aren't 9 to 5 anymore. Second, it did take some extra effort to get these revenue channels motoring, but these days the payoffs are exponentially higher than the effort required to maintain each channel.

By the end of this chapter, you'll know as much about my life as I do. Just don't get any crazy identity theft ideas. I'm here to help you on your own personal working-less and earning-more journey, not out-source my life to you. So let's get started with real estate investing. Let me show you how to make some solid passive income without having to marry into the Trump family.

Passive Strategy 1: Investing in Real Estate

If your goal is to build skyscrapers, commercial properties, or condominium complexes, you've come to the wrong subchapter. Do I believe you can get rich from building cities, strip malls, and gated communities? Of course you can. But these are what I call working-more and earning-more strategies. You're not going to erect a 12-store commercial strip mall three days per week. It's going to take blood, sweat, and tears to turn that patch of dirt into a thriving shopping complex. Again, if that's your dream, more power to you. But this section covers how real estate investing can become a fantastic passive supplemental income channel.

My wife and I own a two-family home approximately 5 miles from our primary residence. If you're not familiar with two-family homes, basically they look like regular houses but have two front doors. Aside from sharing a driveway, the two tenants lead separate lives. In most cases, even utilities are separated to avoid disputes over air-conditioning usage and lights left on too long. I truly see two-family homes as a great introduction to passive rental income. First off, two tenants are more manageable than running an entire apartment building. Second, you can earn some nice positive cash flow to supplement your other income channels. Third, you're starting small while you learn the ropes before deciding to invest in additional rental properties.

Over time, I've come to realize a successful two-family rental comes down to three basic factors:

- You've got to buy the right place.
- You need to make sure the place will attract tenants.
- You have to choose the right tenants.

What follows is your guide to getting it right when it comes to buying the place, fixing it up for renters, and choosing tenants. Nail these three factors and you'll see the cash roll in month after month. Overlook even one of the factors and your investment will turn into a money pit quicker than a baby snatches just about anything you put in front of him.

The Buying Game

Home buyers are traditionally emotional about their decisions. Why do you think "curb appeal" is so important? You'd be amazed how often someone claims their price range is $300,000 to $350,000 only to stretch and buy a new place for $425,000. Living beyond your means in a primary residence is a personal decision, but it's a killer when it comes to investment properties. The first rule of buying an investment property is to remove emotions completely. Your cash flow success comes down to one question: does the math work? In simplest terms, if rental income is lower than your mortgage payments, you've got an investment dud on your hands. Okay, so you can still make money if the place appreciates, but why not go for positive cash flow in the meantime?

Let's bring the buying game to life with an example. We're going to break down a $500,000 two-family home to see whether the investment makes fiscal sense. To arrive at our answer, we'll need to consider down payments, interest rates, anticipated rents, and of course costs associated with owning a property.

Buying a $500,000 Property

Down payment (20%)	$100,000
Mortgage interest rate	6.5%
Monthly mortgage payment (includes taxes and insurance)	$2,800/month
Monthly rent: apartment #1	$2,500/month
Monthly rent: apartment #2	$1,800/month
Landscaping/snow removal	$150/month (avg.)
Water bill	$30/month (avg.)
Maintenance and repairs	$400/month (avg.)

So how does this property stack up? On the income side, you're earning $4,300 per month in rental income. On the expense side, you're spending $3,380 per month on average if you add together the mortgage, landscaping, water bill, and repairs. On the surface that comes out to $920 per month in cash flow or $11,040 per year in passive income. If your goal is to earn $100,000 per year while working less, you just found over 10 percent of your annual income target with minimal day-to-day work required.

Of course an inability to rent one or both apartments could swallow up that positive cash flow, but let's keep things optimistic. If there are a few months with a vacant apartment and you only pull down $5,000 cash flow on a particular year, it's not the end of the world in the long run. Besides, in some markets, seasonal or vacation rentals may be more profitable than signing long-term tenants.

> **Less Is More** _____
>
> Beyond your principal down payment, most houses need a little or a lot of work to be truly livable. Depending on the previous owner, you may need to simply slap on a new coat of paint or take on major renovations like a new roof. Remember, the less renovating you need to do, the more you'll make out of the gate.

What you can see right away is that stretching for a $600,000 property could completely wipe out your cash flow, even if you like the more expensive place better emotionally. So when scoping out potential properties, run the numbers and you'll be off to a good start.

The Rentability Game

Owning a rental property without finding tenants is like making a piecrust with no fruit filling. In the buying game, we laid out what it takes for the numbers to work. But there's a second and equally important element in play here. It's called *rentability*. You've got to own a rental property that would actually be attractive to renters. Anticipated rents of $2,500 for apartment one and $1,800 for apartment two means nothing if nobody ever pays those fees.

If you want to fill up your newly acquired rental property, you've got to keep these nine rentability rules in mind. These nine factors cover exactly what it takes to make a renter choose your house and not the one next door:

◆ **Ample indoor and outdoor parking.** Nobody wants to park on the street when they get home from work. A renter's top choice is to pull her car into the garage. She also wants ample driveway parking for visitors.

- **Onsite washer and dryer.** We live in a world of convenience. Washing and drying clothes in your basement is easier than trekking to the local Laundromat. Word to the wise: don't install washers and dryers requiring quarters to operate. Make this a free onsite benefit.

- **Central air-conditioning.** Okay, if you live in northern Canada you may not worry so much about central air-conditioning. However, rental properties with summers that can see sweltering temperatures rent much better when the entire place can be cooled with the flick of a switch.

- **Proximity to public transportation.** Not everyone drives to work. Buses and trains still rule for many commuters. If your renters can walk to a bus or train station, they'll be much happier than needing to park and pay every day after driving to the station.

- **Proximity to town center.** It's Saturday afternoon and a beautiful day. The ability to walk less than a mile into town to check out the shops is a major draw for renters.

- **Reputation of the school district.** For prospective renters with young children, good schools are a must. Even the nicest house won't rent if it forces renters to pay for private school.

- **Crime rates for the town.** Feeling safe at home is a must for renters. Nobody wants to look over their shoulder as they turn the key at the front door. The town, the neighborhood, and your street must all feel safe for tenants.

- **Newness of appliances and fixtures.** Does the sink spew out brown water? Does the water heater make an unsettling creaky sound?

> **Time and a Half**
>
> How can you find out school rankings before you invest in a rental property? Check out www.SchoolMatters.com for the latest data on public schools across the United States. You can quickly learn student-to-teacher ratios, reading and math proficiency levels, and even read parent reviews and ratings.

Does the stove let off a suspicious odor? Renters want to know the appliances and fixtures are in good working order.

◆ **Generosity in repairs, landscaping, and bills.** It's your choice. You can pay for repairs, landscaping, snow removal, and water usage bills or pass one or more of these costs on to the tenant. Before you make your decision, check out what your competitors offer to level the playing field.

The Renting Game

You bought a place with great cash flow, and you've paid attention to the nine rentability factors. Now you've got a great place ready to fill with the perfect tenant. This is the last major factor in winning the rental game. Pick the right tenants and the cash flow is yours. Pick the wrong tenants and your entire game plan can blow up in your face.

Here are five points to keep in mind when selecting a potential tenant. Master the art of picking the right tenant and you're on your way to becoming a landlord who works less and earns more.

◆ **The credit score.** Pay attention to that credit score. People with great credit rarely miss monthly payments. Those with poor credit often have excuses (i.e., the dog ate my rent).

◆ **Debt problems.** Debt factors into the overall credit score, but you'll want to look at it closely. How much debt someone carries gives you a sense of how they handle their money. The more debt they carry, the more money problems they could have and the more likely they could miss a payment or two.

◆ **Prior landlords.** Calling prior landlords is much better than references from a tenant's friend. You'll get the honest scoop on whether the tenant pays on time, how noisy she is, and how demanding she is when it comes to wanting repairs.

◆ **Pets and children.** Renting to a family often entails children and pets. Keep in mind that little ones and cuddly dogs scampering around the house often lead to damages. You'll want some carefully worded language in your lease to cover this issue.

◆ **Your gut feeling.** Beyond credit scores, debt, references, and children/pets, never underestimate your gut feeling on a prospective tenant. If something feels wrong, don't be afraid to walk away and look for someone else. It's better to lose a month or two of rent than lock in the wrong person for years to come.

Passive Strategy 2: Selling Products and Information Online

Everybody is knowledgeable about something. Everyone has a few subjects they know more about than the average person. That's why you get all excited when your favorite subject appears on *Jeopardy*. You're watching with your family when all of a sudden Alex Trebek announces the categories for Double Jeopardy. Science Fiction or Medieval Monarchies pops up and you immediately know you'll run the table, trounce your family, and win kudos for the rest of the night.

Successfully selling products and information online is similar to dominating in your favorite *Jeopardy* category. You need to find a subject that you know more than most people and then get those people to pay for what you already know. But how do you figure out the right topic? It starts with a list of all the subjects in which you have above-average knowledge. This would be a sample of 12 topics from my list:

Human resources	Dating and relationships
Baseball	Career development
Public speaking	Stand-up comedy
Exercise and fitness	Baby's first year
Getting organized	Elder care
Real estate investing	Freelance writing

This probably looks like quite the eclectic list. But you'd be amazed how many subjects you master through school, working, hobbies, and life experiences. Notice I'm not claiming to be a world-renowned expert in these subjects. I'm just fairly confident that at a dinner table with 12 random strangers I'd be one of the most knowledgeable in these subjects. In fact, I'd be knowledgeable enough that these dinner guests might be interested in what I have to say on these subjects. They might be interested enough to even pay for that knowledge (but let's not get ahead of ourselves quite yet).

Now it's your turn. Stretch yourself a bit and come up with 12 subjects you'd smile over if they appeared as categories in Double Jeopardy:

1. _____   7. _____

2. _____   8. _____

3. _____   9. _____

4. _____   10. _____

5. _____   11. _____

6. _____   12. _____

Now it's time to narrow the playing field. Nobody is going to take me seriously if I write about stand-up comedy, baseball, human resources, public speaking, and fitness all in one shot. You've got to hone in on the right subjects by asking two questions:

> Which of these 12 subjects am I most knowledgeable about?

> Which of these 12 subjects am I most passionate about?

Whichever of the 12 subjects appears on both lists is the right place for you to start making money online. For me, the answer would be dating and relationships and career development. That's really how I figured out that my company Bold Road should be all about helping people reach their potential in career, love, and life.

Once you've nailed your subject matter choice, you're only five steps away from earning passive income online. Rest assured there are hundreds of books devoted to online marketing, so consider this your introduction to the subject. If this whets your appetite, by all means pick up a copy of *The Complete Idiot's Guide to Online Marketing* and you'll really hit the ground running.

Step 1: Write an E-Book or Record a CD

This is not as hard as it might seem. I wrote my first e-book about mastering online dating. The key is to pick a topic that's not too general and not too specific. An e-book on dating advice would be too broad to attract an audience, whereas an e-book on meeting 37-year old bankers from Kentucky would be a bit too narrow.

I brainstormed 10 major points I wanted to make in the e-book, and this became my table of contents. For example, I included a chapter on choosing the right Internet site, writing an attention-grabbing profile, making first contact with prospects, and planning the all-important first date. You crank out the e-book and convert it to Adobe Acrobat, otherwise known as a PDF file. Don't let this technical jargon scare you. For less than $300, you can download Adobe Acrobat and easily convert your Microsoft Word e-book into an Adobe file people can download.

Your other option is to record the e-book as a CD for downloading, but I find that requires a few more technical gadgets (i.e., recording software). So if you want to keep it simple and get the passive income going, start with the downloadable e-book. You can always create additional products, including that downloadable CD, once you've taken that first step.

Step 2: Build a Website

What's that you say ... you don't know the difference between HTML files and JavaScript? The good news is you don't need to know the difference. Do you remember those freelance sites I mentioned like www.Guru.com and www.Elance.com? Well, for approximately $200 you can outsource the design of a professional website, including a newsletter, e-book downloading capabilities, and integration with an eCommerce site to collect your earnings.

In fact, all I had to do was pick a website designer and e-mail over the text for my e-book sales page.

What ... you've got writer's block and can't come up with the text for a website sales page? Throw in another $50 and you can outsource the writing, too. That's $250 total to turn your idea into a fully functioning, professional-looking, passive-income-generating website. Just be sure to pick someone with expertise in your field. Otherwise it will be difficult for them to generate catchy sales language.

Time and a Half

Building a website with newsletter capabilities, eCommerce, and e-book downloading functionality might seem like a lot of work. Luckily there are sites out there like www.1ShoppingCart.com that bundle all these services together for one low monthly price. You can even negotiate for your website designer to integrate sites like 1ShoppingCart directly into your site. Your friends will think you're a technology wizard when they see all the bells and whistles on your site.

Step 3: Draw Traffic to Your Website

Maybe you've heard a thing or two about search engine optimization (SEO). When you go to Google and search a term, the results that come up on the front page have been optimized for Google's search engine. These sites have the right key words and content which tell Google they're most relevant to what you, the information seeker, want to see. Most website designers will automatically optimize your site as part of the outsourcing deal. The only problem is it can take six months or more for Google, Yahoo!, and other search engines to notice your site among the millions out there. That's six months of waiting around for your first sale.

Who has time to wait six months for some dough? This is a book about working less and earning more! You can draw traffic to your site immediately through two programs: Google Adwords and Yahoo! Search Engine Marketing. These two programs offer paid search results—those sites that typically appear across the top and down the side of your search results. You can be up and running in three simple steps:

1. Google or Yahoo! will help you determine the most relevant key words for your e-book. Examples for my e-book might be online dating, Internet dating, and online profile.

2. When people search the terms related to your e-book, your site will show up in the sponsored search results. The more you're willing to pay for each search term, the higher your site will show on the list.

3. You set a daily, weekly, or monthly budget and Google or Yahoo! will automatically remove your ad once enough people have clicked through to your site to meet your budget limit.

Ask Jeff _____

So how else can you draw quick website traffic without paying the big search engines? Consider signing up affiliates who sell for you. All you have to do is offer an enticing commission on each sale to build a motivated virtual workforce. People you never met will be working around the clock to sell your stuff.

Step 4: Build an E-Mail List Through Freebies

Now you've got an e-book written, a website up and running, and hot prospects clicking on your site. Your goal is for one of two things to happen every time someone visits your site. Goal 1 is they buy the e-book. Goal 2 is they provide their e-mail address so you can stay in touch. Marketing gurus will tell you it can take as many as seven e-mail contacts with someone to drive a purchase decision.

So how do you capture the e-mail address? You make a deal. You offer a valuable freebie—for example, 10 never-before-revealed secrets about meeting your mate online—in exchange for the e-mail address. Folks type in their e-mail and automatically receive the report. This helpful freebie gives them a taste of what you have to offer and hopefully drives them back to your site to make a purchase down the road. Now that you have their e-mail you can stay in touch regularly and continue to tempt them with additional passive products and services as you create them.

Fear Busters _____

Who has time to e-mail thousands of people to draw them into your site? It's easier than you think. Most newsletter programs are fully automated. You can craft seven e-mail communications and instruct the program to send them out to captured e-mail addresses one by one over two weeks. You'll seem like a great pen pal when in reality the newsletter program is doing all the work for you. Sites like www.1ShoppingCart.com can fully automate this concept for you.

Step 5: Sell Increasingly More Elaborate Products

The real working-less, earning-more dollars roll in when you can master the step approach to marketing. The idea is to convince your online customers to buy increasingly more elaborate (i.e., more expensive) products and services. You started with a freebie to get them in the door. Now you've sold them an e-book for say $19.95 or $39.95 (if you included a few bonus reports).

As long as you create quality products, people who buy from you and enjoy your work will beg for more. Why do you think best-selling authors do so well with their follow-up books? So as the e-book sales start rolling in, take some time to think about related products you could sell for repeat business. For example, I could offer an online dating master workbook for $49 to complement my e-book. I could even invite e-book buyers to an exclusive tele-seminar for $129 to teach them insider online dating tips right over the phone. You get the idea ... you're slowly stepping your customers up the staircase to more and more elaborate products. The higher you take a customer up the staircase, the more you'll earn and the less you'll have to work.

Passive Strategy 3: Earning Royalties and Residuals for Life

Which scenario sounds better to you?

♦ You create something original and get paid one flat fee for your time.

♦ You create something original and get paid one flat fee plus life-time royalties based on customer sales.

Call me crazy, but I'll take the second scenario and those lifetime royalties. I get plenty of bills shipped to my door every day; why not mix in a couple of royalty checks while I'm at the mailbox?

There are two primary ways you can take a ride on the royalty train. The first is writing a book and the second is licensing an invention. Okay, so you could also write a hit song. But the odds of coming up with this summer's must-hear pop song are somewhere in line with winning the lottery. Let's instead focus on book-writing and inventions, two great ways to work less and earn more through royalties.

Why Read a Book When You Can Write One?

Hoping to score big with the next *Da Vinci Code* or *Harry Potter* is not what this section is about. Write one of those best-sellers and you can follow it up with the *Complete Idiot's Guide to Never Working Again for as Long as You, Your Kids, Grandkids, and Their Kids Shall Live.* This section is about writing a book that earns enough to make back your advance and leads to royalties for years to come.

When you sign a book deal, you typically earn money on two fronts:

- You get paid a flat fee or advance to deliver the manuscript by a certain deadline.

- You earn royalties per book sold after you earn back the advance.

Ask Jeff

So how do you come up with an idea for a book? It doesn't just hit you on the way to work. Start with the same exercise we did for e-books. Think about subjects you're both knowledgeable and passionate about. Then take it one step further and consider topics for which you have an established platform. Publishers are more likely to give a book deal for a dating book to someone who has a dating radio show, writes a relationship blog, or has published a magazine article on meeting a mate.

Let's say you received $10,000 as an advance to write a manuscript. Let's also say you'll earn approximately $1 per book sale in royalties. This means after the first 10,000 books are sold you'll have covered your advance ($1 times 10,000 books = $10,000) and will now make $1 per book from 10,001 through the total number of books sold. Your deal might even escalate to $1.50 or $2 per book if you achieve certain sales targets.

This fits in perfectly with our working-less, earning-more goals. Sure you may have to bust your rump roast to produce 80,000 words in three months. But after the legwork is complete, the work drops down and you kick back waiting for those royalty checks. Write a few books and you can start receiving multiple royalty checks to keep the passive income rolling in. Of course, you can also hit the promotional circuit, both online and offline, to create some buzz and drive even more sales.

The big question is whether to go the fiction or nonfiction route. If you're confident you have a fiction best-seller in you, who am I to stop you? But by and large I believe the nonfiction route is a better place to start for one reason only. When submitting a nonfiction book proposal, you only have to write one sample chapter plus the table of contents. Fiction proposals require a completed manuscript. In the spirit of working less, I'd much rather write just one chapter and see whether a publisher is interested before cranking out the rest of the book. But that's just me.

If you really want to hit the ground running on a book deal, I highly recommend *The Complete Idiot's Guide to Getting Published* by Sheree Bykofsky and Jennifer Basye Sander. You're probably thinking I'm just recommending this book because I'm a *Complete Idiot's Guide* author, too. The reality is I followed this book page by page to score my first book deal for Dating, Inc. That was long before I ever met the fine folks at Penguin and started writing this book. Sheree and Jennifer can walk you through all the basics of getting published, including ...

- ◆ Choosing a book idea.
- ◆ Submitting your proposal to publishers.
- ◆ Landing a book contract.
- ◆ Working effectively with a book publisher.
- ◆ Continuing to write books for years to come.

Why Wish for a Solution When You Can Invent One?

When my wife and I had our first baby, our eyes were suddenly opened to a world of baby products. One walk through the baby superstore and we were amazed at all the products for safety, teething, toilet training, diaper collection, playing, riding, sleeping, rocking, and soothing. At first glance it seemed every possible product had been invented.

Over time you start to see holes in the baby products industry. Your baby attempts to pick up a fork and spoon and fumbles them both through his little fingers. You begin to visualize a new device, maybe a fork on one end and a spoon on the other. Okay, so this is not my strongest invention idea, but you didn't really think I'd share my invention A-list with the world. (Not before I have a patent anyway.)

My wife and I would go to dinner with other new parents, and everyone seemed to have an idea for a new baby product. Unfortunately, 99.96 percent of these ideas never get beyond the idea phase. People are too busy, too lazy, or too overwhelmed by the thought of bringing a new idea to market.

If you've never heard of licensing an invention, you're missing out on one of the easiest ways to work less, earn more, and score some solid invention royalties for years to come. Here's how it works in five straightforward steps:

> **Time and a Half**
>
> If you're looking to master the invention process without getting a Ph.D. in inventing, I highly recommend www.InventRight.com. In a straightforward three-hour audio tape, you'll learn 10 steps to license a deal and collect royalties. Stephen Kay, the audio-CD author, has made millions from invention licensing deals, and he breaks it all down for you in this CD.

1. **The Idea:** New ideas probably hit you every day. Capture these ideas in a notebook or on your BlackBerry and research them. See what's out there already to get a sense of the originality of your idea.

2. **The Provisional Patent:** The United States government hit on a brilliant idea with provisional patents. Rather than spending thousands on a full-blown patent, you can spend a few hundred to file a provisional patent. This gives you one year to exclusively bring your idea to market. Visit www.USPTO.gov for online access to a provisional patent application.

3. **The Prototype and Benefits:** You'll need a visual representation of your idea, either a drawing or mock-up. Plus you'll need to clearly explain the consumer benefits of your invention in one

page or less. If you can't draw or sketch to save your life, go to one of the freelance sites we discussed earlier and outsource this work. Just be sure to sign a confidentiality agreement with the chosen vendor to protect your idea.

4. **The Manufacturer Search:** Go to the store where your invention would be sold. Look for companies selling similar products. These are your best bets to contact and see whether they're interested in a deal with you. See how these companies attract customers. Could some of their sales strategies also apply to your idea?

5. **The Licensing Deal:** You're basically cutting a deal that says the manufacturer will take on the financial risks of producing the actual product and will therefore collect anywhere from 90 to 95 percent of the revenue. You'll only see 5 to 10 percent, but that's not too shabby considering you spent next to nothing to bring the idea to market. This just might be the time to bring a lawyer on board to cut the best deal possible.

Doubling and Tripling Your Income Through Joint Ventures

When you go into business for yourself, it's only natural to believe it's you against the world. You see a competitor in your field and you want to stomp them out quicker than a bug crawling across your kitchen floor.

I was extremely leery of competitors when I first launched Bold Road. I figured competitors were all about ...

◆ Stealing my ideas to put me out of business.

◆ Stealing my clients to put me out of business.

◆ Stealing my business plan to put me out of business.

What's the theme here? I figured my competitors had one goal and one goal only ... to put me out of business as quickly as possible and make more money for themselves.

Over time I learned the exact opposite lesson. The world is a pretty big place, and plenty of people want to partner together to find that coveted win-win situation. There's room for everyone. If Google and Yahoo! can coexist, so can Bold Road and a few competitors. So I changed my tune and went from fleeing competitors to seeking them out. My open-minded approach paid big dividends right away:

♦ We shared best practices to make all of our companies more successful.

♦ We confronted business obstacles by looking for solutions to our most pressing challenges.

♦ We brainstormed new product ideas for each other's businesses to help everyone grow bigger.

 Ask Jeff _____

How do you find joint venture partners? If you're an author, www. Amazon.com is a great place to start. Once your book is listed, you can easily see similar books recommended by Amazon in your genre. This becomes your hit list of joint venture partners to contact. Industry associations are another great lead for making new friends, sharing best practices, and ultimately launching your own joint ventures to earn more than ever before.

Most importantly, we entered into joint ventures to make more money collectively. The perfect example involves my first book, *Dating, Inc.* When the book first hit the shelves, I did my share of PR to drum up interest. From newspaper interviews to television appearances to radio segments, I talked up the book whenever the opportunity presented itself. It was a whirlwind experience and paid off with book sales, but I was still just one person.

Then I learned about a way to exponentially improve book sales. What if I could convince 20 authors in my field to all promote each other's books at the same time? Now I'd reap the benefits not just of my own PR efforts but those of 20 additional authors. The net result was watching *Dating, Inc.*, climb to #158 on Amazon. Not too shabby for a guy without the last name Grisham or Rowling.

If you want to successfully go the joint venture route, remember three simple rules:

- **Be helpful.** Joint venture deals by their very nature mean both parties win. If you come across as being in it for yourself, you'll look like you're just using your partners. Before even approaching a partner, make sure your idea is a win-win, not a win just for you.

- **Be transparent.** As you discuss deals, be honest about your goals, approach, and expected outcomes. Joint venture deals fall apart when one person has a hidden agenda.

- **Be communicative.** Share the learnings from your joint ventures. Don't get all secretive and hold those learnings close to the vest. Show you're a true team player by saying exactly what went well and what could have been improved for your next go-around together.

Follow these three rules and the joint venture partners will be knocking down your door for a chance to work less and earn more right by your side. Now get out there and start earning some passive income. Your free time is counting on you to make it happen.

The Least You Need to Know

- Active income requires your presence while passive income can be earned while you sleep, eat, or hit the gym.

- A rental property with negative cash flow is equivalent to running up debt on your credit card.

- Everybody knows something people would pay to learn; the key is packaging it up to sell that information online.

- It's an earning-more home run when you can sign a contract that pays you up front for your services and also offers royalties or residuals for a job well done.

- Finding business partners for joint ventures is a great way to exponentially grow your income without growing your time spent working.

Part 3

Integrating Personal Productivity and Financial Secrets into a 10-Year Success Program

Choosing the right income stream is only half the battle in achieving a working-less, earning-more lifestyle. Your own personal productivity and money-management skills contribute heavily to your success. Part 3 of this book is about building a 10-year program to lock in your new lifestyle for years to come.

We start by covering various productivity shortcuts that can convert you into an efficiency whiz. From there, we break down the role your spending habits play in helping or hurting your earning goals. Finally, we put it all together into a 10-year, 10-step success program.

9

Shortcuts to Super-Charge Your Productivity

In This Chapter

◆ Admitting how you work today as a first step in improving your productivity

◆ Organizing a workspace conducive to getting the job done

◆ Being productive every day, month, and year

◆ Mastering the nine life categories to lead a productive life

◆ Freeing up your time through outsourcing to focus your efforts on earning more

◆ Staying away from time wasters that can sabotage your day before it even starts

Do you consider yourself productive? If I asked you to provide a list of everything on your plate right now, how long would it take to produce such a list? Ten seconds? Twenty minutes? Two days? You'll get back to me?

So far we've covered five great ways to earn more and work less. Freelancing, consulting, running a business, earning passive income, and even staying in your job can all be avenues to earning more than ever before. The working-less part can be trickier. If it takes you three hours to do something I can accomplish in one hour, I'll hit my working-less target that much quicker. For many on the working-less, earning-more journey, the hours spent on the job come down to productivity. This becomes of paramount importance if you become your own boss. Manage your time effectively and you'll be king of the castle. Get caught up in time wasters and efficiency traps and you just might end up working more hours than in your old life.

This chapter is all about laying the groundwork for efficient, effective working. You start with an honest look at how you get stuff done today. I then help you tackle your workspace to make sure it's set up to optimize working conditions. From there, I help you build a model that can help you be productive every day of the year. Finally, I cover the most common efficiency traps that sabotage even the best-laid plans.

An Honest Look at How You Get Things Done

When I first left corporate America, my former colleagues were united in one thought. "You'll never get anything done at home," they chanted in unison. My peers were convinced working from home would rapidly deteriorate into soap-opera watching, household chores, and mid-day naps. While I'll admit to squeezing in laundry between conference calls and even grabbing a cat nap here and there, I categorically deny any knowledge of the latest scandals on *General Hospital*.

In all seriousness, I find this line of reasoning rather amusing. Since when does sitting in an office from 9 A.M. to 6 P.M. guarantee nine hours of uninterrupted, efficient work? In fact, I'd make the claim the average corporate climber actually works no more than five hours during a typical nine-hour slot at work. I'll prove it by mapping out what I bet looks a lot like a typical day on the job:

Time Slot	Activities
9–9:15 A.M.	Late for work thanks to traffic
9:15–10 A.M.	Finish breakfast while Internet surfing
10–11 A.M.	Clear e-mails and respond to voicemails
11 A.M.–12:30 P.M.	Attend weekly team meeting
12:30–1 P.M.	Debrief with colleagues post-meeting
1–2 P.M.	Go to the cafeteria with colleagues
2–2:30 P.M.	Check fantasy scores, call Mom
2:30–4 P.M.	Make edits to a business presentation
4–4:30 P.M.	Hit the vending machines for a snack
4:30–5:30 P.M.	Deal with urgent to-do from your boss
5:30–6 P.M.	Chat with colleagues and pack up

Do the math. You technically were at the office for nine hours, but actual work only got done for five of those nine hours. Do you believe this is the workday of a slacker? Not even close. This just might be the typical workday for a high performer. The fact is most humans simply don't work nonstop for nine hours without a break. It's often the reason for late nights and extra hours on top of the official workday when a deadline is looming. So let's at least agree that if you can spend four nonworking hours in the office, working from home might not be the only scenario capable of distracting you.

It's time to take an honest look at your current level of productivity. We've got to establish your starting point so we can grow together. To help us along, I've created another handy-dandy quiz that can determine where you fall on the productivity spectrum. Answer these 10 questions as candidly as possible and I promise not to judge you. In fact, the more honest you choose to be, the more we can make changes together and truly build a working-less lifestyle that's right for you. Okay, here we go. For each of the 10 questions, circle the choice that sounds most like you.

 Fear Busters

Does the thought of finally getting organized scare you? Relax, even the messiest, most disorganized worker bee can find their way. If you need even more help than this chapter offers, check out www.chaosover.com for even more tips.

Question 1: How many e-mails do you have in your inbox at this very moment?

Choice A: Fewer than 20

Choice B: Somewhere between 20 and 100

Choice C: More than 100

Question 2: Which statement best describes the state of your desk right now?

Choice A: It's so clean it looks like nobody works there

Choice B: A few piles here and there, but fairly neat

Choice C: If the phone rang right now, you couldn't find it

Question 3: Fill in the blank: You have ___ new messages on your work voicemail:

Choice A: 0

Choice B: Fewer than 10

Choice C: Sorry, your voicemail box is full, call again soon

Question 4: How long would it take you to find an important paper document you filed six months ago?

Choice A: Less than a minute

Choice B: It's in one of five places

Choice C: Why bother looking for a needle in a haystack?

Question 5: Which statement best describes your to-do list?

Choice A: It's organized, categorized, and readily accessible

Choice B: It's a bit messy, but you know what needs to get done

Choice C: Who needs a to-do list; it's all in your head

Question 6: Without using the search feature on your laptop, how long would it take you to find a document you saved last year?

Choice A: Three clicks or fewer

Choice B: The document would surface after some file surfing

Choice C: That document is as good as gone

Question 7: If you had 10 things to get done today, when would the most important one happen?

Choice A: Right away

Choice B: Toward the end of the day, but it would get done

Choice C: You make no guarantees

Question 8: You're scheduled to call a colleague at 10:30 A.M. What are the odds you make the call on time?

Choice A: 100 percent, if not higher

Choice B: Pretty good odds unless something comes up

Choice C: Who knew there were points for punctuality?

Question 9: If you and 10 of your colleagues were all asked to complete the same assignment, where would you finish versus your colleagues?

Choice A: Unless someone cheats, you'll be first

Choice B: Middle of the pack, but your quality will be top-notch

Choice C: Do you win any prize money for last place?

Question 10: A colleague asks you to deliver feedback on a document by 11 A.M. tomorrow. How closely do you meet the deadline?

Choice A: Your feedback will be ready to go by 10:59 A.M.

Choice B: Your feedback will be provided sometime that afternoon

Choice C: Please accept your apologies, you completely forgot

How did you make out? Do you have a nice mix of A, B, and C, or do most of your responses fall on the same letter? Let's bring the quiz to life and break it all down.

♦ If you answered mostly "Choice A," I'd consider you an efficiency whiz. You're on time, you respond right away, your inbox and voicemail are under control, your documents are well organized, and people can count on you to do what you say. Think of this chapter as an opportunity to tweak your already efficient ways and incorporate two or three new productivity tricks.

Less Is More

If you already consider yourself an efficiency whiz, don't skip this chapter in an act of arrogant defiance. Even one never-before-read tip can catapult your already productive self forward.

♦ If you answered mostly "Choice B," I'd consider you a fence rider. In some ways you resemble the efficiency whizzes. Maybe you keep a clear inbox and voicemail box, but your productivity lapses in other areas. Perhaps you frequently run late or forget to produce deliverables on time. This chapter is your chance to put it all together and join the ranks of the "Choice A" responders. Get it right and you'll shave hours off your workweek to officially reach your working-less, earning-more goals.

♦ If you answered mostly "Choice C," I'd consider you a messy Marvin or the perfect candidate to benefit from this chapter. I'm imagining it's not news to you that you're often late, your response time lags, your inbox and voicemail are bloated, your documents are scattered like seashells on the beach, and counting on you to do what you say is a risky proposition. Let's just say you've come to the right place, and I hope you'll take the advice in this chapter to heart. There's still time to change your ways and become an efficiency whiz kid.

Regardless of whether you came out an efficiency whiz, fence rider, or messy Marvin, let's all journey together. There's room for everyone on the productivity express. My goal in this chapter is threefold:

♦ **Organizational improvements.** I want to help you get your working space, to-do list, and life under control so that the calls, e-mails, files, and documents in your life don't get in the way of your working-less agenda.

♦ **Productivity enhancements.** I want to help you review how you get stuff done each day to see if there's room to enhance your working style and speed up your output. The more you can get done in less time, the more you'll ultimately make per hour, day, or week on the job.

♦ **Working game plan.** I want to leave you with a practical game plan to approach not only your day, but your week, month, and year so you feel confident you can be your most productive self all the time. This is the ultimate end-state goal where work takes you no longer than it should and your free time begins the moment it's meant to start.

Let's get started on our three-goal journey by analyzing your working space to see if we can make some organizational and productivity improvements.

Creating Your Optimal Workspace

Whether you work from home, in a rented office down the block, or in an office cubicle, an optimized workspace is the first key ingredient to productivity. If your workspace is messy, if your to-do items are disorganized, and if your voicemail box is full 90 percent of the time, then working less is an uphill battle. The messier you get, the steeper the climb.

Lucky for you I'm a Virgo. That means diligence, structure, practicality, and organization are my strong suits. Allow me to take you for a ride on the Virgo train. As you might guess, given our orderly ways, we never miss a stop. Following is your three-part system for creating an optimal workspace.

 Ask Jeff

If you work from home, do you really need a home office? Can't you just set up shop at the dining room table? As someone who works from home, let me be the first to recommend establishing a separate home office. It's hard enough separating your personal life from your business life. Working smack in the middle of your personal life is a recipe for constant interruptions.

Part 1: The Spring Cleaning

You may not want to hear this, but before we can roll out your new organizational system, we need to clean house. If you're looking at a mountain of paperwork and a backlog of open projects, have no fear. We'll tidy up in no time. Okay, so it will take some time, but at least you'll be organized going forward.

All I ask of you is to devote one full working day—about eight hours—to the spring cleaning. Please don't take that to mean you can block off eight one-hour slots over the next three months. We need to get you back to neutral, and that's an impossible task if new to-do items are rolling in over three months while we clean up your messes. So give me just one day and you won't regret it.

Are you ready to give your spring cleaning a shot? Here's what I want you to do. Find a big open space on the floor in your office where we can make a huge pile. No, this is not for a bonfire to say "good riddance" to your to-do items. It's to put everything going on in your life in one place. Here's what I want you to add to this pile:

- All loose papers and documents piled on your desk, on the floor by your desk, and around your office.

- All loose papers and documents stuffed in drawers, cabinets, and closets.

- All unopened mail and packages around your office.

- All to-do lists, Post-it notes, and other papers with pending actions and assignments.

- Your cell phone—that's right, your cell phone—so we can retrieve all the messages from your inbox.

- Your laptop with all the online files, documents, and e-mail messages. Okay, so you don't have to literally throw your laptop on the floor (let's agree to place it lightly on the pile instead).

- Any documents filed away in your filing cabinet if you have one. Just pull the files right out and place them on the pile with everything else.

- Your planner, PDA, BlackBerry, or other device you use to make appointments and stay in touch with the world.

- Your office phone. There's no need to disconnect the cord and toss the phone on the pile. We just want to make sure your unreturned office messages will be part of the process.

- Everything in your briefcase—and I mean everything. You should be able to turn that briefcase upside down, shake it violently, and have nothing come out.

- Anything else lying around your office, at home, or in the car, that might be related to your work.

So how big is your pile? Are you taller than the pile if you stand back-to-back? Don't worry, I've never met a pile I couldn't tame, so I'm sure we can get your work under control. Now it's time for my three-step, foolproof program to complete your spring cleaning.

Less Is More

I really like to minimize my hard-copy paperwork. In fact, if I have the document on my computer, I typically dispose of the hard copy. Why keep extra papers lying around when you can contain everything on one laptop? Just be sure to back up your hard drive to minimize the risk of losing everything.

1. **Review everything and throw out what you don't need.** I won't be surprised if your pile gets cut in half from this step alone. Hopefully that will make your seemingly overwhelming cleanup project more manageable.

2. **Clear out your e-mail and voicemail inboxes.** Start by deleting everything in your e-mail and voicemail inboxes you no longer need. Next, write down who you need to call back and delete those phone messages. I want your voicemail box empty. Finally, respond back to e-mails that are quick-hit and delete those. The only remaining e-mails in your inbox should be open projects or issues you can't resolve in five minutes or less. Ideally, I'd like to see your e-mail inbox down to no more than 20 messages.

3. **Condense all your remaining paperwork down to one list.** You've thrown out unnecessary papers and cleared out your e-mail and voicemail inboxes. Now turn your attention to the remaining papers. First, start one laundry list of open projects that consolidates everything from your to-do lists and Post-it notes. Second,

file the papers you still need in labeled folders that are easily accessible in the future. Do the same exercise virtually with your laptop. File the online documents you still need in labeled online folders.

If you've followed these three steps closely, here's what you should be left with:

- One list of people you need to call back

- One list of all open projects, to-do items, and assignments

- One filing cabinet organizing the papers you still need and one laptop filing system for the online documents you need

- An empty voicemail box and 20 or fewer e-mail messages

Wow, you just went from a bonfire of confusion to two pieces of paper and a filing cabinet! Not too shabby if you ask me. At the very least, I hope you feel a sense of relief over officially knowing what's on your plate. Our spring cleaning is complete; it's now time to implement your new system. By the way, if you really feel the need to hold on to all that old paperwork, stop by the Container Store (www.containerstore.com), pick up one of their creative storing solutions, and pack up what you won't look at for months.

Part 2: The New System

A spring cleaning only gets you so far. If you continue your old habits, that bonfire of to-do items will grow back quicker than ice cream sells out on a scorching summer day. What we need is to give you a new system you can rely on to keep your open projects, e-mails, and voicemails manageable. Remember, you've got a clean, optimized workspace now; let's not mess it up by falling back on old, bad habits. It's time to roll up our sleeves and implement your new system!

I want you to start by reviewing the piece of paper with your open projects, the piece of paper with phone calls to return, and the 20 e-mails in your inbox. This represents your world of open to-do's. Now I want you to categorize this information into the following:

- People, projects, and e-mails you need to deal with this week (or even today)

- People, projects, and e-mails you need to deal with sometime this month

- People, projects, and e-mails you need to deal with next month or later

What we've just done is carved your to-do items into three manageable subgroups. The first group is your most urgent stuff. Ignoring this group is equivalent to disappointing people who are counting on you in the near future. The second group represents open items that need to be on your radar screen but don't require action immediately. The third group covers down-the-road to-do items. Taking action now only muddies the waters on what really needs to get done sooner.

I typically put little ticklers in my planner reminding me when it's time to kick off work on the down-the-road projects. For example, let's say it's January and someone just hired me to give a presentation in October. I'll add a tickler in my planner in August reminding me to start working on the presentation. This way I can completely ignore the presentation for the next six months knowing my planner has a little ribbon tied around its finger to trigger me. By the way, if you absolutely feel more comfortable in the land of hard-copy planners, check out a site like www.AtAGlance.com for a wide range of planners, calendars, and appointment books.

So we've got our people, projects, and e-mails divided into the three categories. Here's how I stay organized throughout the day. Twice per day I set aside time to respond to e-mails, call people back, and reorganize my open project list. This means twice per day I take the following actions:

1. Respond to any quick, new e-mails in an attempt to get my inbox back to 20 or fewer e-mails.

Time and a Half

Here's a quick trick I follow to keep my e-mail inbox under control. Anytime there's a string of e-mail replies on the same subject, I keep only the most recent in my inbox. If I want to see the back-and-forth conversation, then the most recent e-mail contains the string of comments. Sometimes I only need to read the most recent comment to get up to speed on an assignment.

2. Call people back in an attempt to get my voicemail box back to zero messages.

3. Scan any new documents, papers, or mail to take action on the new things rolling in.

If all goes well, these three steps get me back to neutral. Of course, sometimes the e-mails, calls, and new projects can't be completed in these twice-daily slots. When that happens, I add the open items to my to-do list. These open items get added to the lists for this week, this month, or later than this month. Once per week I re-rack the to-do list by ...

◆ Deleting everything that's been completed since last week.

◆ Scanning the list to see if any projects need to change categories. For example, something that was originally slated for next month may have moved up the priority list.

◆ Producing a clean, new to-do list for use going into next week.

That's my system and I'm sticking to it. I hope you find it keeps your life of open projects under control and supports your working-less lifestyle. At the very least, you'll be able to devote less time to organizing your work and more time to getting stuff done on your list. If you want to learn some alternative organizational systems, check out www. LifeOrganizers.com for even more ideas.

Part 3: The Maintenance Program

As you can tell, I'm a bit on the organized side (my wife might call it obsessive), so my maintenance program is rather easy. I clean up throughout the day so my piles, e-mails, and voicemails rarely if ever get out of control. I'm not expecting you to dedicate your life to organization, so let's cover a maintenance program that's a bit less time-intensive.

For the first three months of your new system, I want you to devote three hours per week to getting back to neutral. That means:

◆ *To-do list:* You put any new messes in a small bonfire on the floor, throw out what you don't need, file what you do, and add new projects to your to-do list.

- ◆ *Voicemails:* You clear out voicemails so you have zero new messages and add any new calls to your open call list.

- ◆ *E-mails:* You scan your e-mails, delete what you don't need, respond back on quick hits, and get your inbox back to 20 or fewer messages.

After the first three months, you can drop down to three hours every two weeks. From there, you can even go down to three hours once per month. Over the long haul, the frequency with which you need to get back to neutral comes down to how quickly you get disorganized. Wait too long and the project might feel so overwhelming you'll avoid it entirely. Then we'll be back to square one requiring a spring cleaning again. I'd rather not put you through another one of those. Focus on your maintenance program and we'll leave the spring cleanups to people moving houses and having garage sales.

The Secrets to a Productive Year, Month, and Week

Creating an optimal workspace and managing your to-do list is critical to working less. But how do you take it up a notch and truly deliver a productive year, month, and week? I'm glad you asked because this section will answer that very question. What you're about to learn are seven steps that can lock in a truly productive year in your career and life overall.

My wife and I follow these steps every year, and it's made all the difference in working less and earning more. There's just something about putting pen to paper on your dreams and goals that makes them happen. Isn't that better than meandering through your year with no real sense of whether or not you're on track? As you work through these steps, I know you, too, will feel empowered to make it happen and to take charge of your life.

Step 1: Dream Big and Write It All Down

In December of every year, my wife and I go into separate rooms and write down everything we want to see happen in our lives next year. Okay, technically we might sit in the same room, but we create separate lists. To spur our thinking, we generally brainstorm in nine key life categories:

- *Career:* What do we want to see happen with our business and careers?

- *Love:* What is most important in our relationship with each other?

- *Health:* How do we plan to stay in shape, eat right, and seek medical treatment as necessary?

- *Finances:* How will we manage our money, invest our disposable income, and continue to grow our net worth?

- *Family:* What steps do we need to take to keep relationships strong with parents, siblings, cousins, and of course our little man?

- *Home:* Do we have any plans to move, remodel our home, or make minor upgrades to our living quarters?

- *Friendships:* Which relationships do we want to strengthen, who is fading from our lives, and which new people do we want to meet?

- *Personal development:* How do we plan to better ourselves through hobbies, classes, and self-growth opportunities?

- *Values:* What do we plan to stand for next year in terms of morals, ethics, and personal values?

Did this book just expand way beyond working less and earning more? Yes it did, and I'll tell you why. The end result of working less is the opportunity to live more. So while you may start with goals focused primarily on money-making and career advancement, over time you'll discover all the free time needs to be filled, too. That's when it becomes helpful to start thinking about goals beyond money including family, health, and personal development. We'll keep this section mostly business focused, but I just wanted to stir your thinking a bit and show you these steps can apply beyond just revenue generation.

Step 2: Narrow the List to Major Categories

My wife and I then compare our laundry lists and look for themes. In general, we try and establish nine big-picture goals from the two lists. Why nine? Well, it's our lucky number. We met on January 9 and got married on November 9, and our son was miraculously born on January 9. So around here we tend to think in "nines," but feel free to pick your own lucky number. Here are a few examples of big-picture goals that might make our top nine:

◆ Double our business revenue from last year

◆ Earn a 2 percentage point higher return on our investments

◆ Start one new hobby and take two development classes

◆ Grow our network of friends and contacts by 20 percent

◆ Find another two-family property to invest in

Again, these big-picture goals will span all of the categories, but let's keep it more business focused for now. My wife and I settle on the nine big-picture goals. We then scan the Internet for pictures that depict what we're trying to achieve. For example, we might find a picture of a great-looking two-family house that represents our desire to invest in a new property.

We print these nine photos, frame them, and hang them in our master bedroom. Every night before bed and every morning when we wake, the nine photos serve as constant reminders of the most important goals for the year. You'd be amazed how this system helps seep the goals into your subconscious and keep them on your mind throughout the year. I've gotten so good at this I can be eating a piece of bread while visualizing a juicy steak and almost fool my mind into thinking I've got a piece of meat.

Step 3: Write Actions Required to Bring the Categories to Life

The nine big-picture goals set the vision, but it's the actions that make them a reality. For each of the nine major goals, we brainstorm three to five actions that will make the goals come to life. For example, here are five actions we could take to make the two-family investment property a reality:

1. Set a budget for the price of the house, the down payment we plan to make, and the rental income we hope to earn.

2. Choose two or three towns to target our search based on school reputations, rental histories, and affordability.

3. Find a real estate agent who specializes in two-family properties who can start sending us fresh leads.

4. Book time each week to see new properties and hopefully home in on the one that's right for us.

5. Find a lawyer specializing in real estate transactions who can help us inspect the property and close the deal.

Time and a Half

Here's a quick way to figure out the action steps required to make one of your goals a reality. Simply picture the end state you desire and the roadway will materialize. You'd be amazed how when you see a clear picture of the finish line you can work your way backward until you find the map to make it so.

You can see right away how the vague notion of buying a two-family investment property comes to life when you break it down into the five actions required to make it so. This method also fits nicely into our work-less, earn-more game plan. First, we won't waste time seeing properties in the wrong towns or outside the price range we want to spend. Second, we've crunched the numbers on our desired cash flow so we know buying the right property will fit in perfectly with our revenue goals.

Step 4: Break the Actions into Quarterly Goals

Do the math. You've got nine major categories and three to five goals per category. That's anywhere from 27 to 45 things you want to get done in the coming year. I'm an efficient guy, but even I recognize it's too much for my plate.

That's why we then break all the goals into the four quarters of the year. This way, some goals are slated for January through March while others won't hit our to-do list until October through December. This plan helps make an otherwise insane year of goal achieving that much more manageable. It's really not that hard of an exercise because you'll quickly see goals that require more immediate attention than others.

Step 5: Hold a Planning Session Once per Week

Once per week my wife and I sit down for a planning session. This is where we make sure our plans for the week match what we want to get done. These planning sessions follow three basic things:

◆ **We load in the givens.** We look at any meetings on the calendar, family visits, or other such activities that need to be slotted.

◆ **We pay ourselves first.** From finding workout slots to booking time to focus on hobbies to spending quality time with our son, we carve out time for what matters most to us personally.

◆ **We schedule the nine categories.** Keeping in mind the number of hours we want to work each week, we slot in tasks from our quarterly goals list.

Ask Jeff _____

What if you really want to see your career take off but need some help making it happen? Check out www.MindTools.com for management, leadership, and career training that can supercharge your career. From time management to stress management, you'll find a wealth of resources to hit new career heights.

The weekly planning session is the best way to take control of your week before your week manages you!

Step 6: Track Your Progress and Make Adjustments on the Fly

At the end of every quarter, we check on our progress against our goals. Some goals need to be extended into the next quarter, other goals get revised, and some goals come off the list as the year unfolds. As much as we'd like to master plan the entire year on January 1, things change and you need to make adjustments as you go along.

As a family, we typically follow the "ready, fire, aim" plan. This means that even though it may look like we're extremely organized, we do our best to move toward action quickly and see what sticks. We find that putting something out there and adjusting is a better strategy than waiting until the perfect moment to act.

Step 7: Celebrate Your Success

Because nine is our lucky number, we celebrate our successes every month on, you guessed it ... the ninth of the month. This is our one night for us to reflect on all the wonderful accomplishments, dream about the coming months, and toast to our successes. You've got to take this time out along the way or you'll get caught up in the to-do list and forget to appreciate all you've achieved.

Avoiding the Biggest Time-Wasters and Efficiency Traps

You've taken an honest look at how you get things done. You've optimized your workspace. You've even taken control of your year, month, and week. You're ready to take charge and make the most of your time. That really is the key to working less. All that remains is avoiding some potential time-wasters and efficiency traps that can derail even the most prepared planner. What follows are eight of the biggest traps around. If you can steer clear of these eight efficiency pitfalls, it will be clear sailing as you strive to work less and earn more.

Trap 1: Forgetting to Finish

Working less is not like a game of chess. Your goal is not to slowly advance all of your pawns with none ever reaching the other side. Efficiency goes best with check-offs, and that means getting stuff done.

Multitasking is okay so long as you close out your top priorities. Unfinished phone calls, partially drafted e-mails, and half-completed presentations get you nowhere. Consider closing out the call, then finishing the e-mail, after which you can dive into that presentation with your full attention.

Trap 2: Sabotaging Your Systems

You've invested hours into your spring cleaning, new systems, and maintenance program. The last thing you want to do is give up on your newfound game plan before takeoff. That's a bigger time-waster than never undertaking a new approach in the first place.

If you want to tweak the system laid out in this chapter, go for it. Just settle on one system and stick with it. That's the best way to create consistency and predictability in your workspace and working day.

Less Is More

Multitasking is only worthwhile if you really can do two or three tasks simultaneously as well as one after the other. Juggling too much can lead to dropped balls, and that will put a dent in your efficiency reputation with others. Consider putting down the BlackBerry while you conduct a phone call. Your e-mail recipient and phone call participant will appreciate and notice the undivided attention.

Trap 3: Allowing Unlimited Interruptions

You're supposed to be working on a sales pitch, but the phone keeps ringing, your new e-mail message light is blinking, and co-workers keep popping into your office with quick questions. You look up at the clock and somehow two hours pass without making a dent in the sales pitch.

There certainly needs to be time in your day for phone calls, e-mails, and co-worker pop-ins. But if you've slotted two hours to knock off a sales pitch, then that's your top priority. Respect your schedule and others will, too.

Trap 4: Sticking with Antiquated Technology

Your phone line crackles, your Internet connection is on the fritz, and your keyboard is missing letter "G" and the number "9." It's one thing to save money holding on to old technology. It's something else entirely if that technology is preventing you from getting your job done.

If you run your own business, technology upgrades will be tax-deductible. That means you're technically buying products at a discount. Take advantage of the tax code and buy the equipment you need to be productive.

Trap 5: Meeting for the Sake of Meeting

Every Tuesday your staff holds a three-hour meeting to catch up, realign, and set priorities for the week. These meetings typically start late, begin with idle chit-chat, and meander from topic to topic.

Try shortening the meeting, setting an agenda, and facilitating the group through the key topics. You might seem like a drill sergeant at first, but eventually your colleagues will appreciate your efficient manner (not to mention the extra free time given back by shortening the meeting).

Fear Busters

Does the thought of facilitating a meeting scare you more than camping out alone with no tent? If so, maybe hiring a professional facilitator for an important meeting is the way to go. Check out www.Facilitators. com to hire an experienced meeting facilitator for your next strategic team meeting or offsite retreat. You just might learn something from the pros you can incorporate into your own style. You can also check out the National Speakers Association (www.nsaspeaker.org) to hire a professional speaker.

Trap 6: Letting Your Tasks Prioritize You

You've got six things you want to get done today. You haven't taken the time to prioritize, so you simply dive into what seems most interesting. The day slips away, and you only get to four of your six tasks. Unfortunately, the fifth and sixth tasks really were most important.

Don't choose your to-do items randomly. Check which ones must get done and which ones can wait. Dive head-first into the top priorities. This way if your day slips away too fast, at least you'll have gotten done what needs to get done.

Trap 7: Losing Sight of Your Top Goals

At the beginning of the year you set 9, or 5, or 12 top goals. As often as possible, your working time should be focused on making these goals a reality. Unfortunately, busywork and competing priorities make it all too easy to lose sight of what matters most.

Check in regularly to see how much of your time is invested in the right areas. If months go by without accomplishing anything on your master list, you just might be losing sight of your top goals. Clear your plate of the time abusers and get back to working on what matters most.

Trap 8: Overblending Working and Personal Time

Working less means more time for enjoying life. That's not to be confused with blending your work and personal life. Changing diapers while conducting conference calls and cooking dinner while returning e-mails can lead to problems (not the least of which is accidentally dropping your BlackBerry in the pasta sauce).

If you're planning to work just three or four days per week, block that time off for working and leave the personal stuff for your free days. Setting boundaries early will make it that much easier to be productive both at work and away from the office.

Got No Time? Outsource, of Course!

The eight time-wasters and efficiency traps we just covered can all sabotage your success. But there's one more trap that just might be bigger than the other eight combined. Let's call this mega-trap 9—it's all about outsourcing. You've got to let other folks take on tasks they can do cheaper, faster, and better than you. This point is critical in both your business and personal life if you truly want your time freed up for earning more in less time.

When you think of outsourcing, which of the following pops into your mind first?

Choice A: Customer service reps based in India or China who answer calls from disgruntled big-business customers.

Choice B: A political debate about whether outsourcing costs people jobs or forces them to learn new skills.

Choice C: A newfangled term referring to a recently invented Frisbee game played outdoors.

Choice D: An opportunity to work less by delegating tasks and earn more by refocusing your efforts on what matters most.

If you answered "A," you've spent a bit too much time seeking techni-cal support for your laptop. If you answered "B," it's time to write your governor a letter stating your political views on outsourcing. If you answered "C," I'd like to know how you've heard of a game I just made up. If you answered "D," you're ready to learn the power of outsourcing and what it can do for your working-less, earning-more goals.

In Chapter 6, we talked all about sites like www.Guru.com and www. Elance.com that can help generate new business. What I failed to men-tion at the time is that I also use these sites to outsource tasks related to my business. In recent years, I've ...

- ◆ Paid $150 to build an interactive website promoting one of my books.

- ◆ Paid $50 to receive a detailed spreadsheet outlining all the online dating sites, blogs, and forums in cyberspace.

- ◆ Paid $25 to incorporate newsletter functionality into one of my websites.

- ◆ Paid $75 to enable downloading capabilities after a customer pur-chases one of my e-books.

Add up these four projects and you hit a grand total of $300. Care to guess how long it would have taken me to complete these four tasks myself? For starters, I'd have to technically learn how to incorporate newsletters and e-book downloading into websites. Those two tasks alone could take several hours to learn, let alone actually create on my own. I'm going to very conservatively say it would take three full work-ing days to complete all four tasks.

Regardless of whether I'm making money from consulting, freelancing, public speaking, or book writing, I'm fairly confident I can earn more than $100 per day for those three days. That's all the proof I need that outsourcing makes sense. So why doesn't everyone hand off tasks? I've come to realize it boils down to five main reasons:

- ◆ **Lack of trust.** There's only one person you trust to do a great job—you! Sure you could outsource a project, saving time and money, but there's absolutely nobody out there who can deliver like you. That may be true when it comes to writing a magazine article. You have a particular writing style and sense of humor.

Outsourcing this task may lead to hours of editing and rewrites. That defeats the whole purpose of outsourcing.

What if this article is about endangered penguins living near the North Pole? Might a few bucks for some outsourced research be a good idea? You can still deliver your witty humor and brilliant insights in the finished product. But if someone else can deep-dive on the facts and figures, why not free up your time to make money elsewhere?

♦ **Me-against-the-world mentality.** You want to make it big and have plans to take all the credit when the big bucks roll in. If you outsource pieces of your business, then the credit will need to be shared. The only way to swallow up 100 percent of the glory is to go it alone and complete every business-related task yourself.

First off, who do you seek credit from? If you're starting a business for someone else's approval, you've got to readjust your priorities. Second, do you really think the so-called approval stamps will cease to exist if you outsource a few mundane tasks? It's more likely the opposite will happen. Folks will respect your keen business skills as they watch you manage an outsourced staff toward a successful business.

♦ **Expense micromanagement.** Every dollar spent is another dollar off the bottom line. Why bulk up expenses when you can take on more yourself and maximize revenue? Paying even $10 per hour to take out trash and mop floors can be saved if you simply take out the trash bin and grab a mop before going home for the day.

This argument fails to recognize the most important factor: the value of your time. When you spend an hour mopping, you are saving outsourcing dollars. But what could you have done with that hour instead? If you can earn even a few dollars more than the cost of outsourcing, you've got to pick up the phone and call a clean-up service. Otherwise you're fooling yourself into thinking you're saving money. The reality is you're just blocking yourself from reaching your true earning potential.

♦ **A deeply rooted love for minutiae.** You know some tasks should be outsourced, but you can't help yourself. You just love balancing the books, building websites, researching articles, or setting up meetings. You don't care that these tasks are only tangentially related to running your business. You love these tasks so much you'd do them yourself for free.

Less Is More

When I first started my business, I balanced the books once per month. I've since dropped down to every two months. So whether I do it myself or outsource the task, it only gets done 6 times per year instead of 12. Less book balancing means more time for money-making and enjoying life.

I understand this logic. For some reason I love balancing my business books. I get this strange sense of satisfaction when the math works out, the credits and debits reconcile, and my financial house is back in order down to the last penny. The problem is that this task takes me longer than it would an outsourced professional. I'm also more prone to errors than someone who does this for a living. If you're in this boat like me, it's time to think about outsourcing and getting back to work.

◆ **Lack of outsourcing awareness.** You've been going it alone for so long you never realized you could hand off tasks. You also never realized certain tasks could get done for cheaper than you think. So you continue working with your head down in the sand, missing the chance to take advantage of outsourcing.

If this sounds like you, it's time to make a list of all the tasks on your plate. Then log on to an outsourcing website and see what could get done for you at minimal cost.

Welcome to the Land of Business Outsourcing

So what exactly can you outsource related to your business? Well, a quick scan of sites like www.Guru.com and www.Elance.com reveals that all of the following services can be done by someone else:

◆ Website development and maintenance

◆ Bookkeeping and accounting services

◆ Research and in-depth analysis

- Data crunching and spreadsheet development

- Speech writing

- PowerPoint presentation creation

- Ghost writing for a book

- Technical writing for manuals and handbooks

- Resumé and cover-letter writing

- Prototype creation for a new product idea

- Graphic design and illustration

- Calendar management and appointment setup

- Article and blog writing

- Data entry and transcription services

- Book editing and proofing

The preceding list of 15 is just the tip of the iceberg. I could have devoted this entire chapter to laundry listing everything available for outsourcing. The to-do for you is to think differently about your business, check out the outsourcing sites, and see where you could hand off tasks to free your time for money-making.

Time and a Half

When I outsource a new business task, I like to test two or three vendors on smaller projects before awarding the major assignment. I see what each vendor can do and build trust before investing more money in anyone. It saves you from the risk of rework caused by choosing the wrong vendor.

Your Personal Life Can Be Outsourced, Too

The world of outsourcing quickly expanded beyond just my business. I came to realize I could also outsource tasks in my everyday life to free up more time for running my business or simply enjoying life. You might be amazed to learn all of the following can be outsourced for cheaper than you think:

- Grocery shopping

- Laundry and dry cleaning

- Gift shopping and wrapping
- Babysitting and nanny services
- Breakfast, lunch, and dinner preparation
- Meal cleanup and dishwashing
- Errand running
- Home cleanup and organization
- Landscaping and snow removal
- Home maintenance and fix-it services
- Appointment making (i.e., doctors, play dates)
- Clothing shopping and tailoring
- Party planning and execution
- Computer technical support and maintenance
- Stereo, television, and computer setup and hookup

We're not talking about hiring an expensive butler, a live-in maid, and a personal chef. This is not about living out the life of rock stars and famous actors. The point isn't whether or not you can do all of these tasks. Even if you believe you're not handy and could never spackle and paint a wall, you can learn. The point is how much time are you spending on these daily tasks, what it would cost you to outsource, and how you would spend your newfound free time. I must admit I was skeptical about outsourcing these life tasks. But after looking into the reality of the situation, I discovered ...

- For $12 to $15 per hour, you can hire someone to run errands for you, buy gifts, drop off dry cleaning, and pick up groceries.

- For $12 to $15 per hour, you can hire someone to come to your house once per week for laundry, house cleanup, dishwashing, and light housekeeping.

- For about $50 per day, you can get fully cooked breakfast, lunch, and dinner delivered to your door. That might seem expensive, but how much are you spending today on groceries and eating out?

◆ For $10 to $15 per hour, you can hire a babysitter to watch your kids for a much-needed break or for time to bounce some new business ideas off your spouse.

◆ For $60 to $75, you can hire someone to plow your driveway, shovel your walkway, and dust off your cars. Your lower back will thank you, plus you won't lose productivity the following week thanks to a fever and stuffy nose brought on by prolonged exposure to subzero temperatures.

At the end of the day, it's your life and your business. Whatever you want to keep for yourself is your right. All I ask is that you at least spend the time to look into what can be done by others, both professionally and in your personal life. At the very least, run the numbers to fully understand what your time is worth and how much more free time can be uncovered through outsourcing. This exercise alone could make a huge difference in working less and earning more.

Fear Busters

Does the thought of outsourcing chores and welcoming a stranger into your house scare you more than juggling steak knives? By all means conduct interviews, check references, and even install a video camera if you won't be home. Do whatever it takes to build comfort with those who will make your life easier.

The Least You Need to Know

◆ You've got to take a cold, hard look at how you work today if you want to make some serious improvement.

◆ An optimal workspace is the first key ingredient to getting more efficient and productive.

◆ You can take control of your day, week, month, and year if you apply some time tested efficiency secrets.

◆ Even the best plotted day can get ruined by an efficiency trap.

Chapter

10

Common Cents Money Management and Budgeting

In This Chapter

♦ The connection between money spent and savings lost

♦ Simple budgeting techniques that don't require penny pinching and overly complex spreadsheet tracking

♦ Straightforward wealth-building steps that can double your nest egg

♦ Finding the right balance of earning, working, spending, and saving to achieve your lifestyle goals

Do we really have to talk money management and budgeting in this book? We do if you want to see your new and improved earnings go toward the nest egg and not credit card debt. You see, earning more is a valuable goal only if you can control your spending habits, too. If I help you raise your income from $100,000 to $200,000 but your spending grows from $60,000 to $160,000, what have we really accomplished?

This chapter is all about adding the final piece of the puzzle—spending. So far we've talked all about earning more dollars with less time in the office. But what do you plan to do with all this extra money and free time? Will you go to the mall, blow wads of cash, and end up scraping by to make ends meet? Or will you recognize the role your spending habits play in this equation and master money management, too? Put the credit card back in your wallet, step away from the designer jeans, and get to work on holding on to your hard-earned cash.

In this chapter, I break down the impact your spending habits can have on your long-term earnings. I then cover some basic wealth-building strategies that can double your investment portfolio over time. Next I dive into budgeting. But have no fear; you can leave your pocket protector, calculator, and fancy spreadsheets alone. You'll be learning a simple and straightforward technique to lock in the annual dollars you want to spend. Finally, I put it all together to find the right balance of earning, working, and saving for your particular lifestyle goals.

How Your Spending Habits Impact Your Earnings Outlook

It's time for a one-question pop quiz. No cheating; please keep your eyes on your own paper. Which of the following represents the biggest risk to earning more?

> Choice 1: Choosing the wrong freelance assignment when you first leave corporate America
>
> Choice 2: Starting a small business that fails to get off the ground
>
> Choice 3: Chasing consulting clients who will overwork you and wipe out your working-less goals
>
> Choice 4: Setting up a website to sell e-books only to find out a technical glitch is causing e-book downloading errors
>
> Choice 5: You

Sure, choices 1, 2, 3, and 4 are tempting. Nobody wants to deal with nonmoney-making freelance assignments, failed business ventures, demanding consulting clients, or annoying technical problems. I would argue, however, that these are reversible problems. They actually represent learning experiences that can make your future ventures that much more profitable.

I'm here to tell you that the person in the mirror is your biggest obstacle to actually earning more. That's you I'm talking about, in case you're confused. The very first thing most people do when they come into more money is spend it. That's a surefire way to take all your newfound dollars and flush them quicker than a mouse scampers away at the first sign of a prowling cat.

Throughout this book I've covered how to work less and earn more. The time has come for me to add a third ingredient, your spending habits. That's right, fingernail biting and smoking are not the only bad habits around. Overspending, or what I call rampant consumerism, is also a hard habit to break.

Are you wondering where exactly you fall on the rampant consumerism scale? Lucky for you, I have another quiz that can gauge just how big a problem you face. After you answer these nine questions, we'll break it down to uncover your spending habits as well as what we can do about it. For each question, circle the choice that most closely represents how you would handle each situation.

Question 1: After viewing a television ad for a hot new technology gadget, your next course of action is to ...

Choice A: Buy it immediately.

Choice B: Wait for the price to come down and then buy.

Choice C: Do nothing and get back to watching your favorite show.

Question 2: Your company matches 401(k) contributions up to 6 percent of your salary, so you choose to ...

Choice A: Contribute nothing to your 401(k) account.

Choice B: Contribute 6 percent to your 401(k) account to get the match.

Choice C: Contribute the maximum percentage allowable.

Question 3: You find a gorgeous new shirt on the rack at one of your favorite stores, so you ...

Choice A: Buy it right away without even checking the price.

Choice B: Check the price and see if it's worth the money.

Choice C: Put the item back and head on over to the sale rack.

Question 4: Your bonus is $5,000 higher than expected, so you celebrate by ...

Choice A: Throwing a blowout party that costs $5,000.

Choice B: Saving half the money and spending the rest.

Choice C: Depositing the extra $5,000 in an investment account.

Question 5: You test drive the perfect car, and it's time to negotiate a lease. You ...

Choice A: Go for the top-of-the-line model.

Choice B: Get the basic model plus one or two extra features.

Choice C: Go for the basic model with no bells and whistles.

Question 6: Your boss gives you a 10 percent raise for a job well done; your next course of action is to ...

Choice A: Put this newfound money toward apartment upgrades.

Choice B: Commit half the raise to a rainy-day savings account.

Choice C: Put the entire raise toward savings and investments.

Question 7: You're watching an infomercial claiming to erase 10 years from your face for three payments of $59.95, so you ...

Choice A: Dial immediately and order while supplies last.

Choice B: Research the product to see if it really works.

Choice C: Learn to love your current face and change the channel.

Question 8: Three of your stock picks unexpectedly double in value overnight, so you ...

Choice A: Cash out immediately and head out for a shopping spree.

Choice B: Cash out half the money for a minor shopping spree.

Choice C: Cash out half the money and deposit it in savings.

Question 9: You want to spend $3,000 on your monthly mortgage, but there's a perfect house that will cost $4,000. You choose to ...

Choice A: Go for the dream house and spend the extra $1,000.

Choice B: Meet in the middle and find a $3,500 mortgage house.

Choice C: Keep looking for a house that meets your budget.

Here's what I want you to do: add up your Choice A responses, subtract your Choice B responses, and divide by your Choice C responses. Just kidding. Let's keep things simple. Here's a quick analysis of Choices A, B, and C.

If you answered mostly "Choice A," you fall into the category I would call a *rampant consumer*. You're easily tempted by advertisements, often choose top-of-the-line products, and regularly stretch yourself beyond your spending limits for bells and whistles. You also see newfound money as an opportunity to spend more, not save more.

Less Is More

Don't forget that your 401(k) or Self Employment Pension Plan (SEPP) deposits are before-tax contributions. That means more dollars for retirement and fewer dollars taxed by the government. I'm all for paying my share of taxes, but if the government is going to provide a tax incentive to bulk up my 401(k), I'm going to maximize that benefit.

Ask Jeff _____

How do you really avoid keeping up with the Joneses? I've come to realize that if you can stop the impulse to buy in the moment, your craving will usually pass. The same goes for people impressing you in the moment with their fancy cars and designer clothes. You may feel the impulse to keep up in the moment, but later that night you'll be glad you held on to your money.

If you answered mostly "Choice B," you ride the fence between a spender and a saver. You fall prey to some advertising temptations, see unexpected cash as both a spending and saving opportunity, and will upgrade your life here and there with some unnecessary gadgets.

If you answered mostly "Choice C," don't worry, I'm not going to label you a cheapskate or miserly money watcher. In fact, you have the best shot at making the most out of earning more. You're not tempted by the latest gadgets, you're perfectly happy with baseline product models, and you see unexpected cash windfalls as opportunities to pad your savings, not buy lavish gifts on a whim.

Here's the bottom line: if this book helps you double your earnings, then it's the Choice C folks who will put the greatest percentage of this newfound money into their pockets. Choice A folks will be helping malls, car dealers, and infomercials get rich, and Choice B folks will sit pretty in the middle.

I'm not here to rain on your earning-more parade. I certainly understand the desire to pad your lifestyle when the extra bucks roll in. I just want you to make a conscious decision about your spending habits rather than let mass media make those decisions for you.

Let's really bring this concept to life. Let's say this book helps you earn an additional $50,000 per year. Let's also say you have the opportunity to invest that $50,000 per year in an investment account that will earn a 9 percent annual return. What will this money become in 15 years for our Choice A, B, and C folks?

◆ Choice A responders will spend the entire extra $50,000 every year. They'll own some great cars and travel to some exotic destinations, but the investment account will continue to show $0.

- Choice B responders will invest half the money, or $25,000 annually, while spending the other half. The car and vacations won't be quite as nice as Choice A responders, but the investment account will tally $700,000 in 15 years.

- Choice C responders will invest the entire $50,000 every year in the investment account. They'll still buy or lease cars and go on vacations, but not with the newfound money. In 15 years, their investment account will be worth $1.3 million.

I don't know about you, but I'm willing to wait 15 years for the fancy cars and exotic vacations if it means another $1.3 million in my pocket. How about you?

How to Budget Effectively Without Counting Every Penny

Hopefully you're officially on board with controlling your spending habits to help you truly earn more. You may, however, be in fear of the "B" word. No, I'm not talking about black sheep, balancing checkbooks, or bounty hunters. I'm referring to *budgets*.

I'm going to let you in on a little secret. Effective budgeting is not about penny pinching, splurge control, and complex tracking software. The key is to lock in your spending targets, automate where possible, and get out of your own way. Did I lose you already? Let's break down what I just said:

- **Lock in spending targets.** If your goal is to spend $3,000 per month on the mortgage, don't stretch yourself to a $3,500 mortgage. Buy a place that will lock in $3,000 monthly and you'll lock in this spending category.

- **Automate where possible.** The more savings that get automatically deposited, the quicker your money will grow. On the flip side, the more payments made automatically, the less likely you are to miss payments and inadvertently run up debt.

- **Get out of your own way.** You're going to set a realistic budget in this section, so stick to it. I'm going to make it easy, but you've got to get on board and stop looking for ways to overspend or sneak unnecessary purchases into your life.

Okay, so there's a little more to it than that. What you're about to learn is the easiest, most foolproof, least time-consuming budget in history. Then again, I haven't checked budget plans back in medieval times, so I can't say for sure. Either way, here is a 10-step game plan to gain full control of your money in and money out.

Step 1: Set a Savings Target

I really do believe in paying yourself first. So before I even worry about a mortgage payment or credit card bill, my savings and investment accounts get paid first. For my family, our savings target involves four key steps:

- ◆ My wife and I both max out our retirement accounts based on annual government limits.

- ◆ We choose an amount to invest in our children's 529 college savings plan and make that investment at the beginning of the year before the money can be spent elsewhere.

- ◆ We set an annual savings target and set up a monthly automatic deduction from our checking account into our investment account. This locks in our savings goal from day one.

- ◆ Finally, we move any extra money to a safe money market or CD that holds our ever-growing rainy-day fund.

Step 2: Take a One-Month Inventory

You've paid yourself first, now it's time to take a look at your spending habits. If you already track your monthly spending, then the data is there for analysis. If not, here are two techniques to arrive at a reasonable estimate:

- ◆ Technique 1: Review your checkbook and credit card bills for the last few months to build a yearly estimate.

- ◆ Technique 2: Track your actual spending for one month and then extrapolate out for an entire year.

The goal is to arrive at an expense figure for the year. Let's say you realize you're spending $55,000 annually on all family expenses. That becomes your starting point for making a budget.

Time and a Half

Does the thought of tracking your spending sound about as enticing as sitting in traffic? The good news is you can sync up a program like Quicken to your credit card bill online and download spending activity in seconds. The program will even categorize your spending, giving you a great snapshot of your spending habits in no time at all.

Step 3: Cut the Low-Hanging Fruit

You would be amazed how many unnecessary expenses slip into your bottom line. My wife and I took a look at our spending habits and immediately noticed ...

- ◆ Thanks to a new baby, we hadn't rented a movie from Netflix in six months. We love the service, but putting it on hold immediately saved $15 per month.

- ◆ We were paying $20 per month to rent a bottled water dispenser when Home Depot sold the same model for $99. We quickly traded in the rental unit and made our money back in five months.

- ◆ We had over $1,000 in unused gift cards from birthdays and holidays. Despite shopping at these stores frequently, we had forgotten about the gift cards shoved in our glove compartment.

- ◆ We could pay our car insurance bill quarterly instead of monthly and automatically save a 5 percent processing fee.

I'm not here to say movie rentals, water bottles, gift cards, and processing fees are the key to getting rich. But if free money can be found that won't change your lifestyle one bit, why not go for it?

Step 4: Reduce the Fixed Expenses

There's a big misconception about fixed expenses. I'm going to clear it up once and for all. Too many people mistakenly believe fixed expenses are completely immovable—in other words, whatever you're paying monthly for cable, phone, insurance, etc., that's what you'll be paying for life. The truth is the expense is locked in, but you can reduce that amount through a little detective work. My wife and I uncovered the following fixed-expense savings.

◆ We lowered our homeowners' insurance by $450 per year simply by raising our deductible from $2,500 to $5,000. We realized that insurance is really for fires, hurricanes, and other disasters that wipe out the entire house, not minor repairs from small floods or falling trees.

◆ We lowered our cell phone bills by $40 per month combined when we realized we never exceeded our monthly allowance of minutes.

◆ We reduced our cable, phone, and Internet bill by $1,000 annually by signing up for a package deal with one provider.

Step 5: Make a Few Tough Decisions on Variable Expenses

We've shaved the fixed expenses; now it's time to start looking at variable expenses like clothing shopping, your personal trainer, grocery bills, eating out, entertainment, etc. Rather than attempting to reduce every variable expense by 5 or 10 percent, I recommend first making some tough decisions.

Are there variable expenses you'd be willing to eliminate? For example, could you do without monthly massages and go bimonthly instead? Or would you be willing to only eat out two nights per week instead of four? The idea is to make a few tough decisions you can lock in and get the savings automatically going forward. This is not about eliminating every luxury in your life. So don't start cutting until you're living in a log cabin with no running water. We're just looking for a few concessions that can potentially put thousands of dollars back in your wallet.

Fear Busters _____

All this talk about spending might raise concerns about the dreaded "cheap" tag. Nobody wants friends and family snickering behind their backs as water gets ordered instead of soda to save $2. Rest assured you can find savings without picking up an unwanted frugal reputation. In fact, our philosophy is to be generous with those we love and make cuts in other areas. That way, we never give them a reason to snicker.

Step 6: Arrive at Your New Spending Target

After completing steps 1 through 5, the idea is to arrive at a before-and-after spending target. In step 2, you determined your estimated annual spending. Now you've made some cuts across your fixed and variable categories. How much money did you find? My wife and I were amazed to find over $20,000 in savings from these exercises. More amazing was the fact that we didn't feel even a dent in our lifestyle despite the extra dough in our pocket.

That $20,000 is a powerful number as it fits directly into your working-less, earning-more goals. Think about it: rather than going out and consulting 20 extra days at $1,000 per day, you found the same $20,000 without working another minute. Or rather than accepting four $5,000 freelance projects that could swallow up two months of working time, you get that time back.

Step 7: Lock In as Many Expenses as Possible

I wish I could tell you self-discipline is the answer to your budgeting prayers. Unfortunately, I've come to realize self-discipline only takes you so far. Despite your best intentions, if you don't lock in as many expenses as possible you'll likely overspend inadvertently.

My recommendation is to find and eliminate as many choices as possible throughout the year. Make one decision on each expense and lock it in to avoid the possibility of overspending your target. For example, if you only want to spend $400 annually at your favorite clothing store, buy a $100 gift card to that store every quarter. When the gift card runs out, you're done spending for the quarter.

Step 8: Build a Foolproof System to Prevent Overspending

Not every expense can be locked in. You'll still play a role in your spending for some categories. For example, it's very hard to lock in grocery store or drug store spending. These aren't like your car lease or cable bill, where the monthly amount is a virtual certainty.

That's why I've developed three methods to create a foolproof system to prevent overspending. All three methods work, so pick the one that seems right for you.

1. *The Cell Phone Method:* Your cell phone likely comes equipped with a notepad. For the expense categories you can't lock in, I use the notepad to make a list of the monthly amount I intend to spend in each category. For example, I'll say $450 on groceries or $600 on eating out with friends. As the month goes by, anytime I spend in one of these categories, I simply deduct the amount from the appropriate category in my cell phone. When a given amount hits zero, I stop spending in that category until next month.

   The biggest pro of this system is that I always have the cell phone on me, so my tracking system goes where I go. You can also use your BlackBerry or other wireless device for this method. The main drawback is the potential for human error if you forget to deduct a particular expense.

2. *The Credit Card Notification Method:* Many credit cards come with a special feature where they can notify you when spending reaches certain thresholds. For example, you can receive an e-mail automatically when your credit card charges hit $2,000 for the month. The idea here would be to only use this credit card for those variable expenses you want to monitor.

   The big advantage is you're relying on the credit card company to cut you off when spending hits your self-imposed limit. The downside is you can still charge on the card after the e-mail notification, so you're relying on self-discipline to close your wallet until next month.

3. *The Stored Value Card Method:* Of the three methods, this is probably the most extreme. The idea here is to carry a stored value card for the variable expenses you want to control. Every month you automatically move the amount you want to spend from your checking account to the stored value card account. For example, you might be moving $2,000 per month to the card to cover the various variable expenses you want to control. Once the $2,000 is spent, the money is gone for the month and you can't spend another penny.

   The big advantage is you're guaranteed to hit your spending target. The drawback is the potential for embarrassment when the card gets declined in a busy grocery line. You haven't lived until you've experienced those disapproving stares from impatient folks in a grocery line.

Step 9: Analyze Your Monthly Results

Give steps 1 through 8 a fair shake and then see how you do. Did the anticipated $2,500 in monthly savings materialize, or did you overspend anyway? Take a look to see how closely your targets match your results.

Then make some tweaks to your system until you arrive at something that can work for you. There may be some work up front to hit your stride, but once you do it's smooth sailing and the savings start adding up.

Step 10: Move Newfound Money to Savings or Business Reinvestment

This step is the fun part. I told you my wife and I found over $20,000 annually in savings without adjusting our lifestyle. We could sabotage the entire process and blow it all on a trip around the world. Or we could be money-wise and invest the money in savings or business growth. We typically split the savings between retirement investing and business growth investing. Half the money might go into a retirement account while the other half will go toward learning a new business skill, attending a business conference, marketing a new product, or upgrading our home office technology.

What you do with your newfound money is of course your call. Just promise me you'll make an informed decision; otherwise we just wasted our time in steps 1 through 9. I'll even let you take that trip around the world one year if you promise to invest the expense savings for the next five years.

Simple Strategies to Build Wealth

Let's get one thing clear: this is not an investment book. If you're looking to master investing, I highly recommend *The Complete Idiot's Guide to Investing* by Edward T. Koch, Debra DeSalvo, and Joshua A. Kennon or *The Complete Idiot's Guide to Getting Rich* by Stewart H. Welch III and Larry Waschka. Both books can provide you the soup-to-nuts explanation on amassing a hefty bank account.

My purpose for including a section on wealth building is to make the connection between your investment approach and your working-less, earning-more goals. We learned in the previous section you can save $20,000 or more monthly through smart budgeting. Well, the same holds for your wealth-building choices. The quicker your investments grow, the more money you'll make, and the sooner you can go from working less to not working at all.

If you're hoping to now read about my hot stock tips, I'm sorry to disappoint you. I wish I could tell you who will be the next Google or Yahoo!. Then again, if I could do that I'd be writing *The Complete Idiot's Guide to Clairvoyance.*

Instead, I've compiled six straightforward wealth-building moves you can make, starting today, that have the potential to double your savings. Incorporate these seven moves into your overall investment approach and you'll see that bank account grow as quickly as a new consulting client or freelance project could pad your wallet.

Wise Wealth-Building Move 1: Max Out Pre-Tax Retirement Savings

I'm ashamed to admit it, but for the first five years I worked in corporate America I only socked away 7 percent of my salary in the company 401(k). How did I make this decision? Well, I didn't want to contribute zero and the maximum allowable was 15 percent, so I went for a middle-of-the-road 7 percent. How's that for advanced investment thinking?

My flawed thinking cost me in three distinct ways:

♦ My annual tax bill was higher because I failed to maximize pre-tax savings opportunities.

♦ I lost out on the time value of money by not putting away as much as I could in my early 20s.

♦ I ended up spending the extra money on frivolous nights out with the guys.

Today, my wife and I both maximize our 401(k) and SEPP plans. I'm also entitled to additional pre-tax retirement contributions as a small business owner. Don't think twice on this tip. Jack up your retirement savings to the max and thank me later.

Time and a Half

Choosing where to invest your 401(k) dollars can be overwhelming. Luckily, many 401(k) fund programs now offer lifestyle funds based on your age. As you get older, the money is automatically shifted from higher-risk to lower-risk investments. It's a great way to diversify your portfolio without spending hours analyzing investment options.

Wise Wealth-Building Move 2: Don't Swim in the Credit Card Debt Pool

Credit card debt hurts you in two fundamental ways:

◆ Rates on credit cards skyrocket after trial periods end, and you'll be paying back balances for years to come.

◆ Debt hurts your credit rating, and that means loans for a new car lease or home mortgage won't be as low as for people with better credit.

There's a dirty little game I want you to avoid here. Many people carry credit card debt and also invest in mutual funds and stocks. The thought is that even though you're carrying debt, at least you're thinking about the future and investing some of your money. Do yourself a favor and pay off that debt first. Even if you manage a 10 percent return on the investments, it won't counteract the 15 or 20 percent you're likely paying in credit card debt fees. View paying off your credit card debt as the first and most important investment step you can take. Then move on to picking mutual funds and stocks.

Wise Wealth-Building Move 3: Add Real Estate Investing to the Mix

Diversifying your portfolio applies not just to choosing varied mutual funds. One of the best ways to mitigate risk is to divide your investment dollars between the stock market and the real estate market. This way, if a bear market strikes you can still make money on appreciation of your real estate purchase. On the flip side, if your town hits a real estate dry spell you can still smile as you watch your mutual funds earn a nice return.

Are you a little nervous about plunking down a chunk of change for a house? Let's keep this simple and just talk about choosing to own your house instead of renting an apartment. Consider these two scenarios:

> Scenario 1: You rent an apartment for the next 30 years, spending $2,500 per month on average in rent.

> Scenario 2: You own a house for the next 30 years, spending $3,000 per month on average for the mortgage.

Who is better off? Let's start with the most basic math. The renter is going to spend $900,000 over the next 30 years while the home-owner is going to spend $1,080,000. You might be tempted to say the renter is better off with the extra $180,000 in his pocket. After all, the renter could invest that $180,000 in the stock market and turn it into $500,000 or more over the next 30 years. That's true, but don't forget the government offers a nice incentive to buy a home. The taxes and insurance on the home are tax-deductible, meaning a lower tax bill at the end of the year. So even though the homeowner is paying more in monthly dollars—$3,000 versus $2,500—the homeowner just might be ahead of the renter when tax time comes in April.

Tax incentives aside, the elephant in the room here is the asset gained by a homeowner. At the end of the 30 years, the homeowner can sell the property for $500,000; $1,000,000; or maybe more. What does the renter have to sell? Nothing but some used furniture on eBay.

Wise Wealth-Building Move 4: Understand the Connection Between Your Age and Asset Allocation

Have you ever read an investment book that started by assessing your risk tolerance? You answer 10 questions and find out you're more scared than a turkey two weeks before Thanksgiving. So the book advises you to lean toward money markets, bond funds, and low-risk mutual funds. This way, your principle investment will be secure, you'll make a safe 4 to 5 percent annually, and you'll still sleep at night.

More important than your risk tolerance is your age. By virtue of having more time to invest, 20- and 30-somethings can pick riskier investments than people reaching retirement age. This doesn't mean if you're 25 you should bet your entire life savings on a new eco-friendly organic bathtub cleaner. It does mean you can shift more of your investments toward growth-oriented stocks and mutual funds. As you get older you can slowly shift these investments from growth funds to safer funds that focus on maintaining principle.

Wise Wealth-Building Move 5: Lower Your Tax Bill

Why do so many folks believe the annual tax bill is beyond their control? It's like your accountant or tax software program spits out a number and you just take it at face value. Believe it or not, there are steps you can take to lower your tax bill. This is not about robbing Uncle Sam. This is about taking advantage of tax rules that allow you to keep more of your hard-earned dollars in your wallet. At the very least, consider these three ideas to reduce your annual taxes:

- **Maximize your deductions.** The only thing worse than spending money is spending money without taking the deduction. That's like a double whammy. Take the time to learn which of your annual expenses can be deducted from earnings to lower your tax bill. You just might be pleasantly surprised at all the unexpected expenses allowable as deductions.

- **Sell losses to offset gains.** You're super-excited about the cash windfall courtesy of a lucky technology stock pick. What about that not-so-lucky pharmaceutical stock you picked that keeps dropping in value? Consider selling both in the same year. The loss from one stock can help offset the tax bill from the gain.

- **Hire a professional.** If you're following the advice in this book, your tax situation may be changing dramatically. No longer depending solely on corporate income, you'll be making money through real estate, freelance projects, and/or Internet marketing. Your tax situation will be more complex and just might benefit from a review by a trained professional. At the very least, outsource your tax preparation for one year to see if a tax professional can find tax savings opportunities.

Ask Jeff _____

So where do you find a good accountant who can help lower your tax bill? Do you remember those 1,000 new friends you made in the networking chapter? As you find people working in similar industries, ask them if they know a good accountant. The only thing people like recommending more than doctors and dentists is a good accountant.

Wise Wealth-Building Move 6: Understand the Difference Between Salary and Income

If there's one lesson to take from this book, it's that earning more can be a real challenge when you depend solely on a corporate salary. Sure you can make an extra 4 percent raise every year and a nice bonus. But the progression is steady requiring a long-term career to reach a comfortable retirement nest egg. The income-generating channels we've discussed, from consulting to Internet marketing, are aimed at helping you build wealth. The sooner you start thinking about ways to generate real income—not just earn a salary—the sooner you'll be on your way to working less and earning more.

Locking In the Right Mix of Working, Earning, and Saving

Let's put it all together now. We've talked earning, we've talked working, and now we've talked saving. The end goal is to find the right mix of all three to meet your lifestyle objectives. Taking it a step further, you really want to find the right balance of ...

◆ Hours or days you'll work each year.

◆ Income you'll generate for the time spent working.

◆ Business expenses related to running your business.

◆ Personal expenses related to running your life.

- Dollars you'll put into retirement accounts.

- Dollars you'll put into investment accounts.

- Dollars you'll save toward real estate down payments.

- Dollars you'll reinvest in your business ventures.

- Money you'll have to send to Uncle Sam.

- Money you'll give to charity.

- Money you'll bet on long-shot horses at the race track.

Okay, I threw that last bullet in to make sure you're still paying attention. If there's one thing made clear throughout this book, it's that you can earn more and work less without depending on racehorses and lottery tickets.

There are two ways you can handle this bulleted list:

- You can leave it all to chance and let the chips fall where they may

- You can plan ahead and direct your time and money where you want it to go

As a Virgo, I must admit the planning option excites me more than the "hope for the best" strategy. So let's control our destinies and look at three potential models for dividing up our hard-earned dollars. For all three models, let's assume you'll be working four days per week and generate $200,000 in annual income.

The Squirrel Model

The squirrel is all about piling away as many nuts as possible for the long winter season. In human terms, let's call this the savings-based approach. Your goal here is to see as much money as possible go toward investment and retirement savings. Following is a table of how the squirrel might divide up the $200,000.

	Percentage	Dollars
Business expenses	15%	$30,000
Personal expenses	10%	$20,000
Retirement accounts	15%	$30,000
Investment accounts	15%	$30,000
Real estate investments	5%	$10,000
Business reinvestments	5%	$10,000
Annual tax bill	30%	$60,000
Charitable contributions	5%	$10,000

Less Is More

Remember, the less money you put toward spending and the more money you put toward savings, particularly in those early years, the greater advantage you can take of the time value of money. If there's any way to delay that deep-rooted desire for a top-of-the-line sports car, now you'll have much more money down the road to splurge on luxury items.

The Entrepreneurial Model

The entrepreneur believes the more money reinvested in the business, the quicker it can grow and bring in the real money. So the reward for earning more money each year is bigger and bigger reinvestments in making the business that much more successful. Here's a table of how the entrepreneur might divide up the $200,000.

	Percentage	Dollars
Business expenses	15%	$30,000
Personal expenses	15%	$30,000
Retirement accounts	10%	$20,000
Investment accounts	5%	$10,000
Real estate investments	0%	$0
Business reinvestments	25%	$50,000
Annual tax bill	25%	$50,000
Charitable contributions	5%	$10,000

The Jack-of-All-Trades Model

It's possible your goal is to spread the wealth among retirement, investments, real estate, charity, and everything else going on in your life. If that's the case, then your goal might be to send a few dollars toward every category. Here's a table of how the jack-of-all-trades might divide up the $200,000.

	Percentage	Dollars
Business expenses	10%	$20,000
Personal expenses	10%	$20,000
Retirement accounts	10%	$20,000
Investment accounts	10%	$20,000
Real estate investments	10%	$20,000
Business reinvestments	10%	$20,000
Annual tax bill	30%	$60,000
Charitable contributions	10%	$20,000

One of these three models may sound right to you, or possibly some combination of the three. Perhaps you're an entrepreneurial squirrel or a jack-of-all-trades entrepreneur. Now's the time to plan ahead and decide where those hard-earned dollars will go throughout the year. Fill in the following worksheet and bring your money plan to life.

Ask Jeff

How do you choose the right model for you? It really comes down to the lifestyle you want to lead. What's most important to you? Is it being generous in the philanthropy department? Is it investing in a business idea and watching it flourish? Figure out your working-less, earning-more goals, and the right balance will flow from there.

My annual income goal is: $_____.

Here's how I'll divide up the income (be sure the percentage totals 100 percent and the dollars total your annual income goal).

	Percentage	Dollars
Business expenses	___%	$_____
Personal expenses	___%	$_____
Retirement accounts	___%	$_____
Investment accounts	___%	$_____
Real estate investments	___%	$_____
Business reinvestments	___%	$_____
Annual tax bill	___%	$_____
Charitable contributions	___%	$_____

This worksheet represents your marching orders when it comes to earning, working, saving, and spending. Now go make this worksheet more than a theoretical or hypothetical exercise. Put it into action and watch your hard-earned dollars work for you.

The Least You Need to Know

♦ Earning more can get outweighed by spending more if you're not careful.

♦ Budgets keep spending under control, but you don't have to become a miserly penny pincher to manage your money.

♦ You can double your investment portfolio without majoring in economics or finance.

♦ Your working-less, earning-more lifestyle depends on finding the right mix of working, saving, and spending.

11

Lifestyle Maintenance: The 10-Year, 10-Step Success Program

In This Chapter

♦ Building a game plan to work less and earn more for 10 years and beyond

♦ Locking in your work-less, earn-more success plan to stay on track

♦ Avoiding the obstacles and pitfalls that could disrupt your new lifestyle

♦ Checking in regularly and making those little tweaks to make your life plan stronger every year

♦ Enjoying the fruits of your labor and making the most of that extra free time courtesy of working less

If only you could achieve a working-less, earning-more lifestyle with the flip of a switch. You'd go to bed on Sunday as a corporate climber and wake up Monday morning working three days per week while doubling your income. If it were that easy, would anyone ever work on Thursday, Friday, Saturday, or Sunday again?

What I've tried to make clear in this book is that working less and earning more takes effort, but it's not an impossible journey. I've covered some of the most promising working-less, earning-more avenues, including consulting, freelancing, running a business, passive income, and even staying in your current job. Now it's time to put all the lessons we've discussed together into an integrated, 10-year success plan. After all, I doubt you're looking to change your lifestyle for just one year.

In this chapter, you start by looking ahead to visualize where you want to be 10 years from now. You'll actually put together the lifestyle you desire so you can ensure your working-less, earning-more game plan mirrors your life goals. You then take your vision and turn it into a 10-step program to lock in the lifestyle you imagine. Finally, I review the obstacles that could derail your success as well as steps you can take to tweak your game plan and stay the course.

Are you ready to journey with me into the future? You may see some gray hair and a few extra wrinkles, but what you *won't* see is a burnt-out employee or an empty bank account. I don't know about you, but I'll gladly take that deal. Hair can be dyed and wrinkles can be moisturized.

A 10-Year Outlook for Your Working-Less, Earning-More Life

I'd like to introduce you to Michelle. Throughout this section, she'll be our fictional corporate America employee looking to transition to a working-less, earning-more lifestyle. We're going to follow her journey from where she is today to where she wants to be in 10 years. As I unpeel the story of her life, I'll also stop to give you a chance to ask yourself the same questions and complete the same exercises as Michelle. By the end of this chapter, both you and Michelle will have mapped out your 10-year success plan. Maybe you'll go to dinner together to celebrate. Then again, fictional friends don't make for the best dinner companions. You might even get a quizzical look or two from your fellow diners when you ask Michelle to pass the bread or offer her a taste of your fresh Atlantic salmon.

A 10-year game plan starts with an honest look at your current situation. Here are some facts about Michelle's life today:

♦ Michelle works at an advertising agency creating copy for fragrance and leather goods product advertisements. She's married with a 2-year-old daughter.

♦ She earns $100,000 annually, including salary and bonus.

♦ She works an average of 50 hours per week all in the office sitting in a 5×8-foot cubicle.

♦ Her two favorite hobbies are working out and taking road trips to new and interesting cities. Unfortunately she only hits the gym three times per month and hasn't traveled in two-and-a-half years.

♦ Michelle's top talents include writing, public speaking, and creativity.

That's Michelle's story today; now how about you? Answer the following questions so we can pinpoint your starting point today. We'll take that information to start building your 10-year game plan.

---

1. What do you do for a living? _____

_____

2. How much do you earn annually? _____

3. How many hours do you work each week? _____

4. What are your two favorite hobbies? _____

_____

5. How often do you participate in these hobbies? _____

_____

6. What are two or three of your top talents? _____

_____

You and Michelle are officially at the starting block. We know what you do for a living, how much you get paid, how many hours you work, what you enjoy away from the office, how often you partake of these hobbies, and those unique talents you have to offer the world. Let's take this information and jump ahead 10 years. First Michelle, then you. Isn't that nice of her to lead the way?

1. How much does Michelle want to be making in 10 years?

    $250,000

2. How many weekly hours does Michelle want to work in 10 years?

    30

Ask Jeff

So how do you figure out the right working and earning targets? Of course it's up to you and the lifestyle you want to lead. Thinking 10 years ahead, a good starting point is to cut your hours in half and double your income. So if you were working 50 hours and making $100,000, shoot for $200,000 in 25 hours.

3. Taking into account Michelle's unique talents and work experience, how could she build a life where she earns $250,000 annually while working 30 hours per week?

    ◆ *Advertising consulting:* Michelle could quit her advertising job and seek fragrance and leather goods companies to hire her as an advertising consultant.

    ◆ *Freelance writing:* She could sign up with freelance sites like www.Guru.com and offer advertising copy services.

    ◆ *Public speaking:* She could offer a seminar on breaking into an advertising career and teach this class at the local continuing education school.

    ◆ *Online marketing:* She could develop an e-book or CD on how to write brilliant advertising copy and offer this product through her website.

    ◆ *Book royalties:* She could cut a book deal with a publisher to write a book about advertising copy that motivates consumers to buy her product.

4. If Michelle had to work only 30 hours per week, how would she spend those extra 20 hours she used to devote to the office?

   ◆ Michelle would hit the gym three times per week and maybe even hire a trainer (thanks to her extra disposable income).

   ◆ Michelle would plan three- and four-day road trips at least once per month to explore new cities. Some would be with her family and others would be with her girlfriends.

That's how much Michelle wants to be earning in 10 years, how many hours she wants to work, how she can earn that revenue given her talents, and what she'd do with all that free time thanks to her working-less, earning-more lifestyle.

Michelle is looking at you again because it's your turn. She just laid out her plans; where will you be in 10 years? Fill in the following worksheet to bring your vision to life.

1. How much do you want to be earning in 10 years? _____

2. How many weekly hours do you want to work in 10 years? ____

3. Taking into account your unique talents and work experience, how could you build a life where you earn your desired income while working your desired hours per week?

Idea #1: _____

_____

Idea #2: _____

_____

Idea #3: _____

_____

Idea #4: _____

_____

Idea #5: _____

_____

4. If you could achieve your income and hours-worked goals, how would you spend those extra hours you used to devote to working?

Idea #1: _____

_____

Idea #2: _____

_____

Idea #3: _____

_____

Time and a Half

What's that you say ... you can't think of your unique talents? I've heard this line of reasoning before. Here's a shortcut to identify those talents in minutes. If you work in corporate America, pull out your last three performance reviews. What themes come up time and again on the positive side? Most likely, these are your unique talents and competitive advantages if you leave your job to do your own thing. If you don't have performance reviews, ask three people who have worked with you for feedback on your strengths.

This is the point when you and Michelle should be feeling good about yourselves. You know where you stand today and where you want to be in 10 years. This should be empowering because the roadmap is written. Unfortunately, if I know you and Michelle, then I'll bet it's not empowerment you're feeling. Instead, it's fear about making this plan a reality. In fact, Michelle easily could identify three obstacles she sees that could derail her 10-year plan:

- Michelle has a baby and plans to expand her family. Taking this risk shakes up her stable, comfortable world.

- Michelle's boss absolutely loves her work and foresees multiple promotions in the future. Leaving now says adios to a sure bet for more money and prestige.

- Michelle is not good at sales and fears the pressure of soliciting her own business. At the advertising agency, projects are sold by the sales force and handed to her when it's time to write advertising copy.

It took a lot of courage for Michelle to open her emotional vault and lay out the fears of going for a working-less, earning-more lifestyle. She's taking your hand now, looking at you supportively, and asking what keeps you up at night when you consider making a change. It's time to open your own vault or at least tell Michelle the combination and she'll do it for you. What are three immediate obstacles that scare you when you think about going for it?

Obstacle #1: _____

_____

_____

Obstacle #2: _____

_____

_____

Obstacle #3: _____

_____

_____

Take a deep breath and pat yourself on the back. Facing your fears is never easy. At least we know what makes you and Michelle believe you could fail on your journey. Now let's turn those obstacles into stepping-stones. What could Michelle do about these three fears?

◆ Michelle's husband works in corporate America and is supportive of her plan. He could agree to stay in his job with benefits for now to give Michelle a shot. If it works out, her $250,000 income will be more than the two of them currently make together.

◆ Michelle has seen the compensation graph. If she stays another 30 years, she will achieve a comfortable retirement. But she's seen co-worker layoffs and realizes nothing is a sure thing. She also wouldn't be starting this journey if she had made peace with a 30-year journey requiring 50 hours per week in her cubicle.

◆ Michelle realizes that freelance sites like www.Guru.com do the selling for you. They send projects that match your skill set, which opens the door for you to impress potential clients. Michelle also knows she can meet mentors through industry associations that can help take the guesswork out of sales.

Fear Busters _____

I urge you to really write down your three biggest fears. Don't ignore the elephant in the room just because you're afraid to face it. If you do that, you'll end up solving the minor obstacles only to keep obsessing about the bigger issues. That's not a recipe for working less and earning more. Get it all out on the table now.

Michelle's fear has officially melted into mush. She's dismissed her three biggest obstacles and cleared the path to begin her 10-year journey. If Michelle can do it, so can you. Take a look at the three fears you wrote down and lay out exactly how you, too, could conquer those fears and join Michelle on the road to working less and earning more.

How to overcome obstacle #1: _____

_____

How to overcome obstacle #2: _____

_____

How to overcome obstacle #3: _____

_____

The vision is set and the obstacles have been turned into stepping-stones. One question now remains: how do you actually make that vision a reality? Knowing where you want to go is a great start, but you still have to get there. It's time to learn the 10 steps required to put it all together and lock in your working-less, earning-more game plan.

Don't worry, Michelle is planning to stick around for the next section. She wants to map out her game plan, too. Together you'll start generating the positive momentum that can make it all happen. I'm guessing Michelle will be added to your holiday card list by the time this chapter ends. Then again, sending a holiday card to a fictional friend can be tricky. How much postage do you need? In lieu of fictional Michelle,

I'm always eager to hear success stories. Send your working-less, earning-more achievements to me at jeff@boldroad.com and we'll celebrate together.

Ten Steps to Put It All Together and Lock In Success

What kind of guy would I be if I left you hanging with just a vision and no way to make it happen? I'm not sure you and Michelle would ever forgive me. So the goal of this section is to bridge you from where you are today to your 10-year success plan. To make this happen, let's take Michelle through the 10 steps. That way you'll know your fictional friend made it. If a fictional friend can do it, why can't you?

Step 1: Get Your Ducks in a Row

I've said from the beginning that working less and earning more is not about quitting your day job on a moment's notice. Anger toward your boss or frustration with corporate bureaucracy are not reasons to storm out of the office without a game plan. Before you undertake this journey, I highly recommend lining up benefits and understanding your spending habits.

Our fictional friend Michelle agreed with her husband that he'd stay in corporate America to ensure family benefits. That doesn't mean singletons are left to fend for themselves. As we've mentioned, organizations like the Editorial Freelance Association offer medical plans at discounted group rates. Just be sure to acquire benefits somewhere to make sure an unexpected illness or injury doesn't derail your plan before it starts.

Michelle and her husband didn't end the planning with medical benefits. They also took a close look at their budget and spending habits. Do you remember our Common Cents Money Management tips from Chapter 10? Don't forget that spending less is another way to earn more. You don't have to do it all through revenue generation. So at the very least, take the following three steps in reviewing your spending habits.

1. **Lock in fixed budget saves.** One example would be refinancing your mortgage at a lower interest to save $300 per month. You make the decision once and the savings are locked in.

2. **Eliminate the extravagances.** Do you absolutely need a top-of-the-line car? Can you live without season tickets to the Yankees for a few seasons? Take a look at your indulgences, cut out a few, and you'll likely save thousands.

3. **Cut back on the must-haves.** We all know food, clothing, and shelter are must-have expenses. But you do have a choice to eat out or cook. You do have a choice to buy the hottest fashions or see what's on sale. You do have a choice of how much you want to spend on rent or a mortgage.

The goal of these three steps is to alleviate budget pressures. The less you can spend during the early working-less, earning-more years, the longer you can stay on the journey without that pull back to your old life. It's when the bank account starts shrinking that you wonder if you've made a terrible mistake.

Step 2: Land a Transitional Assignment

Michelle knew her boss loved her at the advertising agency. That's why she approached her about a transitional assignment. Michelle offered to work part-time for three to six months or even quit and then work as a consultant while her boss searched for a replacement. Michelle's boss was sad to see her go but appreciated the gesture of bridging her to a new hire.

The goal of a transitional assignment is to avoid going from $100,000 to $0 overnight. You'll likely be making less than before, but at least you won't feel pressured to make money. That unnecessary pressure can make you accept undesirable assignments just to stay above water. If you can score a transitional assignment, the pressure is lifted and you're free to implement your 10-year game plan.

Step 3: Drum Up New Business

Landing the transitional assignment is not a sign to celebrate and rest on your laurels. Thanks to her temporary part-time assignment,

Michelle dropped from 50 to 25 hours per week. She could have used her newfound freedom to hit the gym and plan road trips. Instead she jumped right into drumming up new business.

In Chapter 3, we talked about building a network of 1,000 people. This is the time to break out your wedding list, holiday card list, high school yearbook, work Rolodex, and e-mail address book. Start sending out those feelers to see who can help you land business and who knows someone who can help you. This is also the time to join a relevant industry association and/or online site to get your name out there.

> **Less Is More**
>
> Remember, sending a blanket correspondence to all 1,000 members of your Rolodex rarely pays off. Take the time to pinpoint the 25 or 50 top leads and get personal. Reach out to these folks, take an interest in what keeps them up at night, be helpful, and they'll soon return the favor.

Step 4: Bet on the Front Runner

After three months of networking, Michelle has three promising leads. She's been offered an advertising consulting position to help a hot new fragrance get off the ground. Guru.com matched her up with a small ad agency that outsources copywriting to freelancers. She's also met with her local continuing education program and they're interested in a new class on Advertising Copywriting 101.

One way to go would be to accept all three opportunities. Remember, though, that your goal is to work less and earn more. Loading up on work may double your income overnight, but it also may inadvertently increase your working hours. Focusing on the front runner may be a better way to go. That means looking at your three opportunities to see which one poses the best combination of income and hours worked. If you can make $1,000 per day consulting three days per week, that's a better first gig than cranking out freelance ad copy at a rate of $275 per day. Going for the front runner gives you a fantastic taste of working less and earning more. You'll quickly get into the groove of bringing home the bacon without burning the midnight oil.

Step 5: Build the Rest of Your Business

Michelle looked at her three opportunities and decided the consulting gig offered the most promise. The advertising start-up was prepared to offer her $750 per day, two days per week, for six months. With a short-term goal to duplicate her $100,000 corporate salary, Michelle would be earning $6,000 per month for six months, or $36,000. She was more than one third of the way to her goal while working just two days per week.

Michelle then took a closer look at the freelance ad copy gig and teaching assignment with the local continuing education program. Accepting these two opportunities would increase her working time to four days per week total. However, the total expected income from these two assignments over the next six months would only be about $6,000 extra. Michelle would be at her maximum-hours-worked target (four days) but not on track for her revenue target. She'd be at $42,000 total after six months, not $50,000 to be on track for $100,000 over the whole year. Crunching the numbers told Michelle to pass on the freelance writing gig and teaching opportunity to pursue other gigs that could pay more or require less time.

Once you've accepted that first assignment, you need to choose additional work carefully. Remember, you have a weekly hours-worked and revenue target in mind. If you're going to take on three assignments that add up to your weekly hours-worked target, you had better make sure they also supply the revenue you desire. Otherwise you're set up to fail before you even start. It's okay to say "no" to the wrong gig. Remember, saying "no" leaves the door open for a better gig to come along.

Step 6: Undergo a Keep or Dump Assessment

Over the next six months, Michelle did find a higher-paying freelance gig on Guru.com and also a continuing education school in the next town that paid higher teacher salaries. Signing these three deals added up to four days per week of work and $52,000 in revenue. Michelle had locked in her target hours and income for six months. She had chosen wisely.

But we're on a 10-year—not six-month—journey. Halfway through the six months, it's time for a keep or dump assessment. If you do a solid job, you'll likely earn the opportunity for repeat business for all three gigs. But is that a good thing or a bad thing? The answer lies in paying close attention to the actual hours you're working and the actual revenue you're collecting. For example, maybe Michelle's freelance writing gig earns a flat project fee and initially required just one day per week of work. But three months into the project the client became more demanding and lately it's been taking two-and-a-half days of work to collect that same flat project fee. The freelance gig just went from something worth keeping in her work-less, earn-more life to something potentially worth dumping.

At this stage you've got to keep in mind that the only real client here is your lifestyle. It wants certain money earned based on certain hours worked. Some projects support your new lifestyle, while others have the potential to sabotage it. In the midst of your first gigs, you've got to take a step back and run some numbers. Which jobs are worth renewing? Which ones could be kept if the terms are renegotiated? Which gigs are beyond repair and need to be dumped before they drain too many hours?

 Fear Busters

I really don't care for delivering tough messages. My stomach ties in knots and I visualize the worst when I share the bad news. I've realized over time that not cutting ties with an unprofitable client causes more pain down the road than taking action now. Sure, cutting ties is unpleasant, but it's better than keeping a client who runs against your working and earning goals.

Step 7: Blow Out Your Cash Cows

Michelle has realized her consulting gig for $750 per day is her best opportunity by far. It pays the most, the client loves her, and the two days per week are predictable and consistent. The consulting work meets all of Michelle's criteria for working less and earning more. Now it's time to grow this cash cow and milk it for all it's worth.

- Perhaps this consulting client has a second project Michelle could take on.

- Maybe there's another client just like this one that could offer similar or more money.

- Could Michelle be in line for a raise with this client thanks to her outstanding work?

The goal at this stage is to invest more time and energy into what's working. You're not trying to suddenly work 50 hours per week. You're looking to replace those unprofitable clients you dumped in step 6 with more revenue from the cash cows.

Step 8: Brainstorm Cash Cow Extensions

Now that Michelle is expending more energy on her consulting gig cash cow, she begins brainstorming ways to expand the revenue stream. Accepting a second project from the client or asking for more money helps grow the cash cow. But there are also ways Michele could expand the working relationship:

- Michelle could offer advertising services beyond just copywriting, including cutting deals with stations to run the ads or designing graphics to accompany the text.

- Michelle could earn extra commissions by connecting the fragrance company with people in her network of 1,000. For example, maybe one of her contacts is an international fragrance exporter and could bring this product to new global markets.

- Michelle could sell-in additional ad copy work and subcontract this work with another writer. She'd split the $750 daily rate on additional work with her subcontractor, meaning she could earn another $375 per day without doing the brunt of the work.

The goal here is to build around what's already working for you rather than keep selling new business from scratch. The sales cycle is so much shorter when someone already likes your work.

Step 9: Double-Check the Longevity of Your Plan

The 10-year success plan is all about diversification. Expanding your cash cow relationships is not meant to be at the expense of building new opportunities. All you're doing is maximizing the revenue you can earn from your cash cows with the fewest hours worked possible.

Michelle's six-month contract for one project eventually grew into a three-year working arrangement juggling multiple assignments. Still, she realized this would leave another seven years with no work prospects in sight. Again, she chose not to rest on her laurels and sought out other long-term, profitable work that would meet her working-less, earning-more goals. Her efforts paid off:

♦ Michelle landed a book deal on building a one-person advertising consultancy. The publisher offered her a $15,000 advance and 10 percent royalties.

♦ Michelle's alma mater hired her to help redesign the advertising curriculum. They also offered her a permanent paid position on the advisory board to continue shaping the curriculum in the years to come.

♦ Michelle and her husband bought a three-family house. The mortgage and expense to run the house totaled $3,200 per month. Rent collected for the three apartments totaled $4,500 per month. The extra $1,300 each month brought in over $15,000 each year in rental income (not to mention the growing asset in the form of an investment property).

Ask Jeff _____

How do you really know which opportunities are meeting your working-less, earning-more targets? I actually keep a log of the income I'm generating and the hours I'm spending on each revenue channel. I don't panic if one week requires extra time from a client or freelance gig. Instead I analyze the numbers over time to see which revenue streams are most in line with my lifestyle goals.

Does Michelle seem lucky to you? How could anyone really land a great consulting gig, a fantastic book deal, a lifetime advisory position, and a positive cash flow–generating rental property? The answer lies in knowing which work supports your goals and which work sabotages your goals.

You need to treat those four days per week you plan to work like gold. The projects you accept, deals you make, and gigs you take on must add up to your revenue target. Otherwise the numbers don't work and you're in for a lifetime of frustration. When you know which gigs support your goals and which do not, it suddenly becomes easy to decipher good opportunities from bad. You'll naturally start gravitating toward work that can make your working-less, earning-more lifestyle a reality.

Step 10: Circle Back to Your Original Vision

Michelle is now three years into her journey. She's working 30 hours per week, so the hours-worked target matches her original vision. Revenue last year topped out at $209,000. Not too shabby compared to $100,000 for 50 hours per week in her old life. Still, Michelle's 10-year goal is to maintain the 30 weekly hours but grow the revenue to $250,000. Now her job is to review her revenue channels to see where she can find that missing $41,000. She has seven years to find it. Michelle already has doubled her old income and is feeling confident she can make the necessary adjustments to reach her $250,000 target. In fact, Michelle has realized she has a new choice. She can reach her target in fewer days and have more free time or continue to work four days and earn more.

You'll want to check in on your 10-year plan every year. The end-of-year holidays is a great time to dust off the plan and take a gander. Work slows down at the end of December, which frees your time and mind to scan your plan. You'll quickly see where you're on track versus where you need to step it up to make your working and earning goals. Don't underestimate this step. You need to check on your target, lifestyle, and goals every year.

Overcoming Obstacles That Could Derail Your New Lifestyle

If only the 10-year game plan could fly on autopilot! You'd kick back, eat some peanuts, and enjoy your flight. While the steps we've just covered can help to lock in your success, you still need to be wary of some pitfalls and obstacles that can derail even the best-laid plans.

What follows are the six most common pitfalls that aim to sabotage your new and improved working-less, earning-more lifestyle. Tackle these obstacles and it's smooth sailing for 10 years and beyond. Overlook even one obstacle and you'll be forced to take the flight off autopilot to course correct.

Pitfall 1: Accidentally Working More and Earning More

Remember, the name of this book is not *The Complete Idiot's Guide to Working More, Earning More*. We have two goals in this book … to spend less time on the job and bring home bigger and bigger slices of bacon.

Many people mistakenly believe you have to put in longer hours to make the big bucks. When you first make the transition to your new lifestyle, it can be tempting to work all hours of the night in the hopes of hitting it big. It's okay to have that goal, but that's more of a small business start-up mindset—you know, the guys who work out of their garage day and night, tinkering with a computer program until they crack the code. Sure they end up flying private jets and living on yachts three months per year, but they also worked 80 to 100 hours per week to make it happen.

Again, if that's your goal, go for it. Private jets and yachts are nothing to cry about. But this book is about building a working-less, earning-more lifestyle from the very beginning. Chances are if you're working more in your new life than ever before, then something is wrong with your approach.

Ask Jeff

So how do you avoid mixing business with your working-less time? If you work from home, the two have a way of becoming fast friends. First off, I keep my work limited to one room in the house. This prevents business from spilling into the kitchen or living room. Second, I shut down that computer after hours so I'm not tempted to slide back into my office chair.

Pitfall 2: Falling in Love with One Client

I'm not talking about a soap-opera love triangle, although that can ruin a career, too. This pitfall is all about putting all your eggs in one basket. As you tinker with different ways to make money, you'll eventually hit on one client or project that takes off. Rightly so, you'll pour your energy into this cash cow.

This strategy would be like putting your life savings into one stock. Sure you can clean up if the company invents a cure for the common cold. But you also can lose your shirt if they fall under indictment for accounting irregularities.

By all means, go for it when you see a fantastic opportunity. Build the relationship; find product and service extensions you can offer to make even more money. Just don't forget to continue networking and prospecting for new business. This way you'll have something to fall back on when you see the CEO's mug shot on *Entertainment Tonight* after that accounting scandal breaks.

Pitfall 3: Confusing Working Less with Taking Time Off

Take a trip to the mall on a Saturday afternoon. What do you see? How about everyone and their mother grabbing merchandise quicker than the salesperson can stock new products? You'll be reaching to try on a new sweater when some eager shopper will snatch it out of your grasp to upgrade their own wardrobe.

What do malls have to do with working less? Well, hit the same mall on a Monday at 11 A.M. What do you see this time? Probably an empty mall with bored salespeople anxious to help you just to add some excitement to their day. When I first quit corporate America, shopping off-hours was intoxicating. So was running errands, going to the gym, getting haircuts, seeing family, and just about everything else on my to-do list. You'd be amazed how easy it is to fill up a day returning pants, dropping off dry cleaning, picking up some milk, and taking your sister to the airport. Remember, you didn't change your life to become a to-do machine. This is not a vacation. Sure you'll have more vacation days than ever before. But on those three or four days you're committed to working, leave the errands, shopping, and haircuts off your to-do list.

Pitfall 4: Dabbling Without a Cohesive Plan

Should you be a freelancer? Should you consult to Fortune 500 companies? Should you write a book? Should you become an Internet marketing entrepreneur? Should you start a new business? Should you dabble in all of these before making a decision? Maybe not all, but it is okay to experiment a bit and see what hits.

Unfortunately, some folks fall in love with experimenting. They freelance for five months, dabble in book writing for three months, write out a business plan for two months, and set up a website without ever selling a product. Dabbling is intended to find your sweet spot, not avoid deep-diving into truly working less and earning more.

As you know by now, I make money through several channels, including freelancing and book writing, human resources consulting, Internet marketing, and public speaking. But I'm not dabbling in these arenas. Each serves a strategic purpose in helping me achieve my revenue goal for the year.

Pitfall 5: Improperly Structuring Your New Venture

Trust me, you're going to be excited when your new journey begins. So excited, in fact, you may forget to do a little housekeeping at the outset. You might land that first client in 10 days and dive right into making money.

The good news is you found new business right away. The bad news is you may not have taken the time up front to structure your business properly. Now you're taking the client out and paying with your personal American Express card. Your client revenue and your spouse's corporate salary are funneling into the same checking account.

Time and a Half

Finding a good accountant can seem as difficult as choosing the right dentist. Check out www. GoodAccountants.com and let them do the work for you. You tell them the services you need (i.e., small business tax planning) and they find accountants who specialize in those services. About those teeth: maybe flossing a little better will take the pressure off your dentist search.

Before you spend even one penny on starting your new venture or earn one dime from a client, set up your business structure properly. First and foremost, establish a sole proprietorship, partnership, S-Corporation, or whatever structure your accountant believes makes sense for your new life. Second, set up those business checking accounts, get a business credit card, and keep your personal life separate from your business. If you don't take this step up front, you'll be making a new friend all too soon ... the IRS!

Pitfall 6: Earning More and Spending More

The story is all too familiar. Business executive scores a huge promotion and celebrates with a fancier car, bigger house, expensive clothes, and top-tier vacations. Income is up but so are expenses. That means savings are flat or possibly lower.

Look, working less and earning more is not about becoming a miser or living like a minimalist. Although if log cabins, outhouses, and hunting for food are your thing, then more power to you. It's important to understand that earning more comes in two flavors. You can bring in more dollars or you can let fewer dollars out the door in the form of fashion, cars, and gadgets.

As a good rule of thumb, see if you can keep expenses flat as your income grows. Let's say you were earning $100,000 per year in your corporate job and spending $55,000 in annual expenses. Now you're bringing home $150,000 in your working-less, earning-more lifestyle. If you can keep expenses flat, you just uncovered thousands of extra dollars to put in your 401(k) or SEPP plan, to reinvest in your business, or to start a college fund for the kids.

Tasting the Sweet Smell of Success

This is the last section of the book, so I've got to ask you: why did you undertake this working-less, earning-more journey?

- Did you want to double or triple your income?
- Did you want to cut your working hours in half?
- Did you check this book out of the library by accident and figure you'd read it anyway?

For me, working less and earning more serves one purpose and one purpose only … to live more! Otherwise, what is this game all about in the first place? Do you remember earlier in this book when we talked about paying your life first? Now that you're on a 10-year success plan, it's time to bring this concept to life. When we first talked about paying your life first, you probably viewed it as a hypothetical. But if you've followed the steps in this book, then you really have established a life with one, two, or three extra days off every week.

So how are you going to spend that time? This is your opportunity to flip back to that chart you completed in Chapter 1 on how to spend your hours. That's how you imagined a week in your life. Well now you really do have that free time, so bring your imagination to life.

Fear Busters

Some people are afraid all this free time will be a curse. You'll get bored, you won't know what to do, and you'll feel underutilized. Let's break that mindset right now. Working does not define you. It's what you do away from the office that builds your legacy. See your newfound freedom as a blessing and put that time to good use. Your life will thank you.

Every Sunday I really do pay my life first by mapping out my week. Work is at the bottom of the list on my schedule. Sure, I know I'll need to block three or four days for money-making, but not before the living gets prioritized. So before I lock in that first conference call, client meeting, or freelance writing slot, I ...

◆ Block off three to four workout slots at the gym.

◆ Slot in time to play with my son and take him to music class.

◆ Make dinner reservations for date night with my wife at that new Italian place downtown.

◆ Hold two hours for piano lessons to see if I can finally master major and minor scales.

◆ Plan my next trip to Boston to visit my grandmother living in assisted living.

You get the idea. These are the most important life experiences to me. They represent the reason I sought a working-less, earning-more lifestyle in the first place. If you don't pay your life first, one of two things happens:

◆ **You end up working full-time anyway.** It's not intentional, but extra calls, e-mails, and meetings will infiltrate any free hours you offer up. Fail to slot in the gym, date night, and play dates, and you'll fall back on working instead.

◆ **Your free time gets swallowed up with errands, television watching, and miscellaneous to-do's.** The dry cleaning will always need to be picked up, that leaky faucet will need to be addressed, those bills don't pay themselves, and dinner certainly doesn't cook itself (although a crock pot, one of my favorite ways to cook, comes pretty close). There's a time and place for to-do's and household chores, but that time is not every waking hour you're not working. Go ahead and slot in running your household, just not at the expense of living more.

It's time to put pen to paper one last time and commit to what it really means to you to work less and earn more. For me, the answer is simple:

Working less and earning more means shifting my life balance to what matters most, mainly my family, my friends, my hobbies, and my unique life experiences that grow and nurture my development.

What about you? Why do you want to work less and earn more? Write it down now, look at it often, and let it guide you when you wonder what this journey is all about.

Working less and earning more means ...

_____

_____

_____

_____

You've got your marching orders. You've got the tools and resources you need to be successful. You've got a 10-year plan to lock in your success. Now it's time to start your journey and enjoy the ride. Remember, the sooner you get to work, the sooner you'll be working less! So get on that Bold Road and take charge of your life today!

The Least You Need to Know

- Building a working-less, earning-more lifestyle is not a one-time event; it takes a long-term game plan to succeed.

- There are steps you can take today to lock in your success for 10 years or more.

- Pitfalls abound that can derail your working-less, earning-more lifestyle, but you can avoid them.

- You've got to check in regularly and make adjustments as necessary to make sure you're still on track to achieve a working-less, earning-more lifestyle.

- Now that you're officially working less and earning more, make the most of that extra free time and don't forget to live more!

Appendix A

Recommended Reading

I hope you've enjoyed *The Complete Idiot's Guide to Working Less, Earning More*. May it be the start of your personal journey toward building the life you've always imagined!

If you're thirsting for even more reading material on this subject and related topics, I recommend the books listed in this appendix.

Allen, David. *Getting Things Done: The Art of Stress-Free Productivity*. New York: Penguin Group, 2001.

Clyatt, Bob. *Work Less, Live More: The New Way to Retire Early*. Berkeley, CA: Nolo, 2005.

Drake, John D. *Downshifting: How to Work Less and Enjoy Life More*. San Francisco: Berrett-Koehler Publishers, Inc., 2000.

Ehrenreich, Barbara. *Bait and Switch: The (Futile) Pursuit of the American Dream*. New York: Owl Books, 2005.

Eker, T. Harv: *Secrets of the Millionaire Mind: Mastering the Inner Game of Wealth*. New York: HarperCollins, 2005.

Ferriss, Timothy. *The 4-Hour Workweek: Escape 9-5, Live Anywhere, and Join the New Rich*. New York: Crown Publishers, 2007.

Langemeier, Loral. *The Millionaire Maker's Guide to Creating a Cash Machine for Life*. New York: McGraw-Hill, 2007.

Levy, Mark. *Accidental Genius: Revolutionize Your Thinking Through Private Writing*. San Francisco: Berrett-Koehler Publishers, Inc., 2000.

Merson, Len. *The Instant Productivity Toolkit: 21 Simple Ways to Get More Out of Your Job, Yourself, and Your Life, Immediately*. Naperville, IL: Sourcebooks, Inc., 2005.

O'Bryan, Pat. *Your Portable Empire: How to Make Money Anywhere While Doing What You Love*. Hoboken, NJ: John Wiley & Sons, Inc., 2007.

Robinson, Joe. *Work to Live*. New York: A Perigee Book, 2003.

The Ultimate Small Business Guide: A Resource for Startups and Growing Businesses. New York: Bloomsbury Publishing, 2004.

White, Jennifer. *Work Less, Make More: Stop Working So Hard and Create the Life You Really Want!* Hoboken, NJ: John Wiley & Sons, Inc., 1998.

Zelinski, Ernie J. *The Joy of Not Working: A Book for the Retired, Unemployed, and Overworked*. Berkeley, CA: Ten Speed Press, 2003.

B

Technical Support

Throughout this book, particularly in the sidebars, I've noted various websites that can help you work less and earn more. Perhaps you're thinking, "Why can't the author compile all of the recommended websites in one handy-dandy location?"

Today is your lucky day. Following is a list of all of the websites mentioned in this book, as well as a few others thrown in to help you out along your journey.

www.1ShoppingCart.com

Offers e-commerce and e-business software solutions for companies looking to market their products and services online.

www.ABIworld.org

Sponsored by the American Bankruptcy Institute, this website can match you with a professional bankruptcy advisor to help get you back on your feet.

www.AtAGlance.com

For those who still prefer hard-copy organizing, the site offers a range of planners, appointment books, and calendars.

www.Batna.com

Teaches the ins and outs of negotiation, including communication tips, training materials, and advice for closing the deal.

www.BirthdayAlarm.com

Never miss another birthday with automatic reminders sent to your inbox for everyone's special day.

www.Blackberry.com

Provides mail access, IM capability, Internet connectivity, video recording, phone calling, an organizer, and GPS capabilities all in one.

www.BookExpoAmerica.com

Brings together the largest gathering of publishers, authors, editors, and other industry professionals for an annual conference.

www.Bplans.com

Helps business start-ups create online business plans in no time with sample plans, a template to fill out, and online expert advice.

www.Business-Value.com

Business Value Research, Inc., can provide an objective and unbiased appraisal of the value of your business to help you set the market as you consider prospective buyers for your business.

www.ChaosOver.com

Len Merson, founder of Productivity Concepts, Inc., provides useful tips to manage information flow and organization.

www.DrDemartini.com

A great starting point for tips, tools, books, and motivational seminars for your personal and professional development.

www.eLance.com

Provides an online workplace where individuals and businesses can find and hire people to work on freelance assignments.

www.Entrepreneur.com

Offers tools, a search engine, message boards, and resources for owners of small businesses.

www.Facilitators.com

Offers experienced meeting facilitators to help run smooth meetings and offsite team retreats.

www.FinishRich.com

Supplies how-to financial educational tools and resources to help people save and manage money effectively.

www.FlexPaths.com

Offers a web portal that connects individuals and employers interested in flexible working arrangements.

www.FourHourWorkWeek.com

Serves as companion website to the best-selling book by Timothy Ferriss and includes steps to plan a mini-retirement and calculators to determine the cost of your dream lifestyle.

www.GLGroup.com

Consists of eight industry networks where experts can join and provide consulting expertise on an as-needed basis.

www.GoFreelance.com

Connects freelancers and employers through a freelance work exchange and database of available projects.

www.GoodAccountants.com

Online service that helps individuals, small businesses, and corporations find suitable accountants.

www.GoToMeeting.com

Provides online presentation, product demonstration, interactive training, and meeting collaboration services.

www.GoToMyPC.com

Gain instant access to your computer files, program, and e-mail network from any web browser or wireless device.

www.Guru.com

The world's largest online marketplace for freelance talent to connect workers and employers locally, nationally, and globally.

www.iFreelance.com

Connects buyers and providers on freelance services through a database of available projects and freelance talent.

www.InventRight.com

Provides tools, resources, and how-to guides to help inventors get new product ideas to market.

www.iPhone.com

Offers one integrated solution for telephone, e-mail, maps, Internet, organizer, weather reports, camera, and calendar.

www.iPrint.com

Personalized online printing services to cost-effectively produce business cards, brochures, mailing labels, and more.

www.LifeLock.com

Offers a proactive solution to prevent your identity from being stolen before it ever happens to you.

www.LifeOrganizers.com

Provides tips to get your home, office, finances, and life in order while reducing clutter.

www.LinkedIn.com

Offers an online network of over 17 million business professionals to help expand your personal relationships.

www.MediaBistro.com

Provides opportunities for media professionals to meet, network, share best practices, find jobs, and further their education.

www.MindTools.com

The career-oriented site offers training in management, leadership, and career advancement to make you a high performer.

www.MomCorps.com

Flexible employment site that matches employees who have opted out of traditional jobs with employers willing to take on flexible working arrangements.

www.Money.aol.com/calculators

Provides free finance calculators for mortgage planning, loans, college savings, retirement calculators, and more.

www.Mozy.com

Offers secure, remote access to all the files, photos, documents, and music on your hard drive for a monthly fee.

www.MyPartTimePro.com

Matches freelancers looking for part-time or flexible arrangements with potential employers.

www.Nsacct.org

The National Society of Accountants can help your business with everything from tax preparation to financial planning and even management advisory services.

www.NSASpeaker.org

The National Speakers Association is a great place to find a professional speaker or facilitator for your next meeting.

www.Outsourcing.com

Offers information on the outsourcing process from needs assessment to choosing a vendor.

www.PracticalChaos.com

Read Judy Martin's blog, tips, and advice for finding work/life balance in a world that never sleeps.

www.SalesGenie.com

Sales lead provider to help open doors for businesses looking to drum up new business and find new customers.

www.SBA.gov

U.S. government website established to provide training, financial advice, and resources for start-ups and business owners.

www.SchoolMatters.com

Website for parents looking to research public schools including average test scores, school reviews, and student/teacher ratios.

www.SCORE.org

With over 10,000 former executives as members, this organization provides free in-person and e-mail support for aspiring start-ups.

www.The-EFA.org

A professional resource for editorial specialists, including job listings, networking events, and group medical benefits.

www.TheOutsourcerZone.com

Includes articles, an outsourcing directory, and information on how outsourcing can impact your business.

www.USPTO.gov

United States Government–sponsored website where you can download patent applications for inventions and ideas.

www.WorkOptions.com

Site specializing in offering scripts, advice, and how-to items for getting a flexible work arrangement approved by your employer.

www.WorkSpaces.com

Your one-stop shop for setting up an efficient virtual office from home including desks, chairs, bookcases, and accessories.

www.WritersMarket.com

Companion website to the popular book, the site helps locate markets for publishing your work, helps track manuscript submissions, and offers advice for aspiring writers.

Index

F

X–Y–Z